www.brookscole.com

www.brookscole.com is the World Wide Web site for Brooks/Cole and is your direct source to dozens of online resources.

At *www.brookscole.com* you can find out about supplements, demonstration software, and student resources. You can also send email to many of our authors and preview new publications and exciting new technologies.

www.brookscole.com
Changing the way the world learns®

Rethinking Disability

PRINCIPLES FOR PROFESSIONAL AND SOCIAL CHANGE

ELIZABETH DEPOY
University of Maine

STEPHEN FRENCH GILSON
University of Maine

THOMSON
BROOKS/COLE

Australia • Canada • Mexico • Singapore • Spain • United Kingdom • United States

THOMSON

BROOKS/COLE

Executive Editor: *Lisa Gebo*
Assistant Editor: *Alma Dea Michelena*
Editorial Assistant: *Sheila Walsh*
Technology Project Manager: *Barry Connolly*
Marketing Manager: *Caroline Concilla*
Marketing Assistant: *Mary Ho*
Advertising Project Manager: *Tami Strang*
Project Manager, Editorial Production:
Katy German

Print/Media Buyer: *Doreen Suruki*
Permissions Editor: *Kiely Sexton*
Production Service: *Shepherd, Inc.*
Copy Editor: *Jeanne Patterson*
Cover Designer: *Roger Knox*
Printer: *Webcom*

Printed in Canada
1 2 3 4 5 6 7 07 06 05 04 03

For more information about our products, contact us at:
Thomson Learning
Academic Resource Center
1-800-423-0563
For permission to use material from this text, contact us by:
Phone: 1-800-730-2214
Fax: 1-800-730-2215
Web: http://www.thomsonrights.com

Library of Congress Control Number:
2003104123
ISBN 0-534-54929-2

Brooks/Cole—Thomson Learning
10 Davis Drive
Belmont, CA 94002
USA

Asia
Thomson Learning
5 Shenton Way #01-01
UIC Building
Singapore 068808

Australia/New Zealand
Thomson Learning
102 Dodds Street
Southbank, Victoria 3006
Australia

Canada
Nelson
1120 Birchmount Road
Toronto, Ontario M1K 5G4
Canada

Europe/Middle East/Africa
Thomson Learning
High Holborn House
50/51 Bedford Row
London WC1R 4LR
United Kingdom

Latin America
Thomson Learning
Seneca, 53
Colonia Polanco
11560 Mexico D.F.
Mexico

Spain/Portugal
Paraninfo
Calle/Magallanes, 25
28015 Madrid, Spain

We dedicate this book to our students, Linda Alley, Kimberly Anderson, Allyson Ashe, Brittney Astbury, Kristy Bronsberg, Edward Andrew Caron, Jr., Andrea Doody, Kristen Labrie, Kathryn Spearing, Jenifer Spinney, and Brandy Walsh. Their questions, suggestions, comments, and requests for clarity and explanation helped us to make improvements which we believe have added substantially to our work.

I would like to thank my writing colleague, partner, and best friend—Liz. Without her words of encouragement, critique, support, and playfulness this work would not have been possible.

Brief Contents

Contents

Chapter 7

Legitimacy   86

Chapter 8

Legitimacy from Without   90

Chapter 9

Legitimacy from Within   106

SECTION 3

Fashioning Communities   119

Chapter 10

The Traditional Stance: Putting the Cart Before the Horse   121

Chapter 11

Professional Stance Through Explanatory Legitimacy: Putting the Horse Back Where It Belongs   139

Chapter 12

A Social Justice Model of Community Legitimacy 152

Preface

Within the past two decades, academic conceptualizations of disability have shifted and significantly changed. Different from the view of disability as a medical deficit, contemporary scholars have advanced theories of disability as socially and culturally constructed and thus influenced by multiple socio-political factors (Albrecht, Seelman, & Bury, 2001). Although rich in academic interchange, the discourse about disability is riddled with disagreement about the nature of disability, its definition, the language describing it, and its meaning to those who are considered disabled. Because of the disagreement and conceptual confusion, discussion and action that are meant to advance the understanding of the lived experience and to address the needs of disabled people often are confused, delayed, and even derailed.

We therefore developed Explanatory Legitimacy Theory and wrote our book for several reasons. Within the academic arena, we sought to provide a theoretical framework in which multiple perspectives of disability are seen as conceptually clear, purposive, and useful; to build on current disability studies literature and theory by placing disability in the context of human diversity; to link disability theory with lived experience; and to make the history, current foundation, and application of disability scholarship accessible to students, providers, policymakers, and others concerned with promoting communities in which all people including those with disabilities can experience social equality.

Another purpose for writing this text is to provide a theoretical framework for action. By examining disability as a category system that is built on values about why people act and look like they do and experience what they do, an expanded framework for understanding, acceptance of perspectives, and collaborative action can occur.

Finally, we believe that the Explanatory Legitimacy Theory extends beyond disability to all human categorization and response. Our approach is one in which perspectives that are seen as conflicting can be reconceptualized as complimentary and collaborative. Through the lens of Explanatory Legitimacy Theory, we posit a structure in which descriptive, explanatory and axiological approaches to human phenomena can be clarified and distinguished as the basis for conceptual clarity and collaborative discourse. Explanatory Legitimacy Theory is therefore comprised of those three elements (description, explanation, and axiology), with the value element as the critical and dynamic determination of who is a member of a specified category and who is not and how members should be met with social responses.

The book is divided into three sections. Section 1, "Foundations," takes us back in history to examine how what we know today as disability was conceptualized and met with community, family, and individual response. In Section 2, "Explanatory Legitimacy Theory," we detail our definition of an analytic approach to disability. We then apply Explanatory Legitimacy Theory in Section 3 "Fashioning Communities," to improve the lives of all individuals, including those who have, currently do, or will fit the criteria for being disabled.

Although published, our work is always a work in progress. We hope that this book not only contributes to the scholarship of disability, but also serves as a set of thinking and action strategies for social and professional change.

Acknowledgements

Many people have made contributions to this work. We are especially grateful to Heather McDuffie for her willingness to listen to our thinking, for her substantive research, and for her major contributions to Chapters 2 and 3. We also acknowledge the helpful comments, suggestions, and guidance of Allison Carey, Temple University; Lynn Gitlow, Husson College; Nancy Kropf, University of Georgia; Romel Mackelprang, Eastern Washington University; and Penny Seay, University of Texas at Austin.

FOUNDATIONS

Foundations are the structures on which physical, ideological, theoretical, and experiential elements are built. The strength of those foundations determines the efficacy and longevity of what they support. We therefore have chosen to present the foundations for our work first, so that you, the reader, can judge the strength of the ideas, practices, and experiences that have contributed to our thinking.

In this section, we begin with a short introductory chapter that summarizes Explanatory Legitimacy Theory and positions it for use as a lens through which to examine and analyze history and contemporary treatment of what today is referred to as disability. In Chapter 2, we look back in history to gain an understanding of how the diversity of what people do, look like, and experience was explained and treated. Chapter 3 continues our historical gaze and brings us to contemporary times, in which scientific advancement and professional development, capitalism, and diversity emerge as critical factors that shape how disability is determined and addressed.

We conclude Section 1 with a focused examination on disability as an economic phenomenon. Chapter 4 addresses disability as a set of financial benefits and exchanges that have culminated in significant profit centers for many groups involved in disability treatment and related activity. So let us begin!

FOUNDATIONS

Foundations are structures on which to build. Because strong foundations create sound beginnings for development, the chapters in Section 1 provide substantive theory and contextual information on which to anchor our subsequent discussion and analysis of disability. However, foundations are not static. The theoretical lenses through which we look back influence not only what we see but also how we interpret our observations.

In this chapter, we briefly introduce you to our theory of disability, Explanatory Legitimacy Theory, as the analytic framework through which we view and interpret the history of disability. We begin with a brief introduction to the current ideas in disability theory and provide an overview of our organizing theoretical framework for understanding disability in today's context. This information is essential to understanding both the theory on which Explanatory Legitimacy Theory builds and the knowledge and analysis presented in this section.

Thus, although we visit the past as a basis for informing our current and future thinking and action, we also look at the past through the analytic lenses that we currently hold.

CURRENT SCHOOLS OF THOUGHT

Explanatory Legitimacy Theory builds on the multiple approaches to defining and analyzing disability that we overview here. Pfeiffer (2002) suggests nine models. However, these perspectives, while diverse, can be organized into two schools of thought (Gilson & DePoy, 2002): disability as a medical-diagnostic phenomenon and disability as constructed. The diagnostic approach to disability places the location of disability within humans and defines it as an anomalous medical condition of long-term or permanent duration (Linton, 1998).

In contrast to this approach and in many cases in opposition to the medical-diagnostic view, the constructed school sees disability as a set of limitations imposed on individuals (with or even without diagnosed medical conditions) from external factors such as social, cultural, and other environmental influences. In some constructed frameworks, the presence of a medical diagnosis is not always a requisite for membership in the "disability" category (Charlton, 1998).

Both categories of thinking provide a forum for rich debate and intellectual dialogue. However, as the discourse expands and is applied to increasingly more fields of study and application, what disability is and is not becomes less clear. As you can see from our brief discussion so far, contemporary definitions of disability are vague and conflicting. Contributing to this conceptual confusion is the failure of current work to distinguish descriptive from explanatory definitions and to illuminate the essential value dimension that places these descriptions and explanations in categories such as "disabled" or "nondisabled."

Another reason for this confusion is the recent appearance of the term "disability." The term and its analogous predecessors (e.g., "handicapped") have been broadly applied to multiple descriptive and explanatory circumstances only in the 20th century (Longmore & Umansky, 2001). Thus, because disability has been considered a category of analysis for a relatively short time, it is not unexpected that no unifying approach to the multiple and confusing approaches to disability definition, causes, and consequences has been advanced. In this book, we attempt to meet that challenge.

DISABILITY: DESCRIPTION, EXPLANATION, LEGITIMACY

We present the key principles and language of Explanatory Legitimacy Theory here only to frame our presentation of foundations. Once you have explored the foundations through the lens of the theory, you will be ready to move on to more detailed and comprehensive thinking about, testing, and applying these new ideas.

In Explanatory Legitimacy Theory, we build on historical and current analyses and debates by defining disability as a human phenomenon comprised of the three interactive elements depicted in Figure 1.1: description, explanation, and legitimacy. Drawing on a rich literature of legitimacy (Jost & Major, 2002), our intent in developing this theory is twofold: (a) to provide an organized framework for analyzing and testing how social, cultural, intellectual, and related trends intersect to shape and dynamically change categorical definitions and subsequent value-based judgments of and responses to groups of humans and (b) to advance guidelines for professional change and social action.

Description	Explanation	Legitimacy
Activity Appearance Experience	Medical-diagnostic Constructed	Judgment Response

Figure 1.1

Three Elements of Disability

Description encompasses the full range of human activity (what people do and do not do and how they do what they do), appearance, and experience. Two intersecting dimensions of description (typical/atypical) and (observable/reportable) are germane to our discussion of disability. The typical/ atypical dimension is a dynamic categorical system of norms and standards of human activity, appearance, and experience. Typical involves activity, appearance, and experience as most frequently occurring and expected in a specified context. Atypical refers to activity, appearance, and experience outside of what is considered typical. For example, typical walking for an adult would consist of a two-legged gait that follows the alternating advancement of each leg, with heel strike preceding toe strike. Atypical walking might involve the use of crutches for ambulation. Observable phenomena include activity and appearance and fall under the rubric of those that can be sensed and agreed on, while reportable phenomena, which we denote as experience, are known through inference only. An example of an observable phenomenon is walking, and an example of a reportable phenomenon is pain when walking.

The second element in our definition of disability is the set of explanations for doing, appearance, and experience. For example, what we just described as the diagnostic and constructed approaches are, in our definitional taxonomy, explanations of doing, appearance, and experience across the life span. Following our example of walking, the medical-diagnostic explanation for pain in ambulation might be the diagnosis of arthritis, while a constructed explanation might be the presence of stairs as environmental barriers that require activity that causes pain.

The third and most important definitional element of disability is legitimacy, which we suggest is comprised of two subelements: judgment and response. Judgment refers to value assessments of groups and/or individuals (sometimes competing) regarding whether what one does (and thus what one does not do) throughout life, how one looks, and the degree to which one's experiences fit within what is typical have valid and acceptable explanations that are consistent with an all-too-often unspoken value set. Responses are the actions (both negative and positive) that are deemed appropriate by those rendering the value judgments. We have selected the term "legitimacy" to explicate the primacy of judgment about acceptability and worth in shaping differential definitions of disability and in determining community, social, and policy responses to those who fit within diverse disability classifications. As we will see in subsequent chapters, many complex factors come to bear on legitimacy, only some of which have been identified in the current literature. Included are social values, economic benefit, cultural beliefs, and power structures (Jost & Major, 2002).

To briefly illustrate, let us return to our walking example and consider two people, Ann and Barbara, both of whom walk with a clumsy gait (observable) and are unable to use an escalator to access the second floor of a public building. The descriptive element in this example refers to the limitation experienced by Ann and Barbara in their mobility and access to the second story. Further, because these gaits are out of the ordinary, walking and access are atypical. Descriptively, then, what both individuals do (walk) and do not do (ascend stairs or an escalator) are atypical and observable.

The next element is explanation. From a medical-diagnostic perspective, Ann's atypical gait and lack of access are explained by a diagnosis of cerebral palsy, and Barbara's are explained by alcohol dependence. From a constructed perspective, however, the presence of the escalator is the explanation for limited access, not the atypical walking due to a diagnostic condition. Note that we still have not identified either person as disabled.

Now we come to the definitional element of our theory: legitimacy. Because we assert that disability is a judgment, who makes the judgment, in what context, and under what set of rules determine membership in the disability category. In this case, both Ann and Barbara name themselves disabled not because of their diagnostic conditions but because of the environment. Ann sees the escalator as the disabling environmental factor, while Barbara identifies social pressures and nonacceptance as the disabling elements in her life. If we look at the medical community, Ann and Barbara are also considered disabled since both have enduring medical-diagnostic conditions that interfere with their "typical functioning." However, if we now look at eligibility criteria for public assistance, Ann is disabled but Barbara is not. The judgment is rendered on the explanation, not the description. Further, the legitimate response differs. Ann can obtain support, and Barbara cannot. In determining who is worthy of public support, the legitimacy or adequacy of the explanation for atypical activity is a function of social, economic, and cultural value. Implicit in the denial of disability status for Barbara is the notion that she is responsible for her own circumstance and thus is not deserving of a support response.

Figures 1.2 and 1.3 compare and contrast the different disability determinations. History and current social trends help us understand how these judgments are made and shape responses to explanations for human activity, appearance, and experience.

Description	Explanation	Legitimacy
Activity: atypical walking and limited access	Medical-diagnostic: cerebral palsy Constructed: escalator or stairs prevent mobility	Judgment from medical community: disabled Social judgment: disabled Response: community support

Figure **1.2**

Ann

Description	Explanation	Legitimacy
Activity: atypical walking and limited access	Medical-diagnostic: alcohol dependence Constructed: social pressures and nonacceptance	Judgment from medical community: disabled Social judgment: not disabled Response: none

Figure **1.3**

Barbara

With this brief introduction to the major theoretical framework of the text, we are almost ready to explore history. Before we move on, however, we need to discuss language so that our use of terms in the discussion of history makes sense.

LANGUAGE

Currently, there is significant disagreement on language that attempts to identify people with disabilities. Person-first language has been espoused by numerous provider groups as well as by some individuals who identify themselves as having a disability. Thus, the term "person with a disability" is suggested to place the personhood before the condition. We do not subscribe to person-first language for a number of reasons. First, we note that such language is used primarily when the descriptor is undesirable. Second, the structure of person-first language implies that the disability is located within an individual. Because we suggest that disability is a value judgment and response based on an explanation of human activity, appearance, and/or experience, the locus of the disability may be both within and outside the individual who is determined to be disabled. Finally, as Heumann (1993) suggests, person-first language is often euphemistic and thus serves to derail the political agenda of disability activists who seek civil rights. We therefore use various terms when referring to people and groups with disability status to reflect the pluralism of our approach to defining disability.

We also want to draw your attention to specific definitions of terms that you will encounter in this book. We have coined two words: "typicality" and "atypicality." Similar to their adjective forms, they denote that which is usual and frequent and that which is odd, different, or infrequent, respectively. We have transformed these adjectives into nouns to denote our view of these constructs as judgments rather than as inherent characteristics of individuals.

Second, a significant part of our theory relies on what we have named "personal stance," by which we mean the unique vantage point from which one observes and interprets. Included are one's experience, knowledge, theoretical lens, beliefs, values, and purposes. Some of personal stance is derived from shared experience, while some is unique to how individuals perceive, organize, and apply their perspectives.

While it may seem like we are splitting hairs or discussing linguistic minutiae, these definitions are important in informing our discussions in the subsequent chapters. Of particular note are two additional nouns that we have developed from their adjective forms: "observables" and "reportables."

Observables are claims that can be verified with directly experienced information, while reportables are inferred or asserted claims. In our lexicon of description, activity and appearance constitute observables, and experience is the element that comprises reportables. These distinctions become critical in legitimacy since agreements on what more than one individual can directly ascertain are often more credible than what is inferred in judging the presence or absence of disability. Consider, for example, the diagnostic category of learning disability. As a reportable, learning disability is inferred from performance on academic tasks. The degree to which performance denotes a disability has been a contentious issue, in large part because the "disability" is not directly observable (Mackelprang & Salsgiver, 1999).

We are now ready to look back in time. As we examine history, think about the contextual influences that contribute to differences in typicality in human activity, appearance, and experience, in explanations for these phenomena, and in how humans with these atypicalities have been met with judgment and responses.

Looking Back: Ancient Greece Through the 19th Century

While the term "disability" or even an analogue of the term was not documented in the historical literature until recently, how atypical activity, appearance, and experience were distinguished from what was typical has been documented as early as ancient civilizations (Longmore & Umansky, 2001). In this chapter, we draw on existing literature to examine how values; the political, economic, and cultural context of the times; and numerous other factors influenced how the atypical was defined and treated.

It is interesting to note that the historical literature, despite contemporary paradigm shifts from a medicalized to a social explanation of disability, still use diagnostic classifications to denote disability. And, while the social, economic, geographic, cultural, and political influences on how these diagnoses have been conceptualized and treated have been brought into the analysis, the historical literature still depends on discussing disability with the language of medical diagnosis. Because medical explanations lack relevance for human diversity in activity, appearance, and experience and because of the poor fit between current medical constructs and historical understandings of the atypical, we approach our discussion with language from Explanatory Legitimacy Theory. If you need to remind yourself about the meaning of terms, we refer you to the glossary at the end of the book.

Chronology

In early Western civilizations, the limits of humanity were drawn at typical body composition (Davis, 1995, 2002; Stiker, 2000). Thus, the classification "human" was not extended to infants, who were at the extreme of physical anomaly in their appearance. However, diverse experiences, such as sensory and mental differences, observable lameness, and illness, were described as human variations. Thus, the *description* of what constituted anomaly was specific to visible sensory and physical activity. Major departures from what was considered typical in vision, hearing, and mobility could therefore be observed and described.

Behaviors consistent with those that are reported, inferred, and labeled today as mental retardation and mental illness were not classified as human inadequacy. Rather, while often feared because of the belief that they were explained by supernatural influences, people who exhibited these behaviors were respected as well (Braddock & Parish, 2001; Davis, 1995; Winzer, 1997). The *explanations* for atypical activity in mobility, seeing, hearing, and so forth were both moral and supernatural. Descriptive experiences, such as "not seeing" or "not hearing," were believed to be caused by the gods for sinful acts, either by the afflicted individual or by an ancestor. Unobserved or unreported traits were often ascribed on the basis of specific impairments (e.g., deafness =unintelligent) (Stiker, 2000), resulting in antecedents of stereotypes. For example, deaf people are frequently assumed to be cognitively atypical only on the basis of their atypical hearing.

While the explanation for human variation in activity at this time was essentially not scientific, Aristotle's early scientific studies and systematic description of the observable world provided a means to identify what was "natural," through what we would consider empirical or at least logical methods. At the same time, Hippocrates' development of medicine and the application of empirical knowledge to treating illness placed rational thought somewhat in opposition to previous mystic explanations of atypical activity. Thus, descriptions and, to some extent, explanations of atypical human activity moved between supernatural and natural, yet the moral element of "the unnatural" still prevailed. For some atypical activity, the moral judgment was one of goodness, but for others, sin was the explanation for the atypicality (Stiker, 2000).

Similar in role and function to our art and media today, myth depicted the value attributed to specific atypicalities (Campbell, Moyers, & Flowers, 1990). In concert with and reflective of the views of legitimate goodness, those with visible atypicalities were portrayed with inferior qualities, while those who acted in a manner consistent with what we classify today as mental retardation or mental illnesses were respected as citizens because they were "possessed" of special knowledge about the will of the gods unknown to the rest of the community (Stiker, 2000).

When atypical activity was explained in immoral terms, the community, not surprisingly, was not amenable to providing support. However, when atypical performance resulted from war injury—where the explanation was known and considered to be heroic—some cities maintained a pension fund to be made available. (To what extent funds were disbursed to women is not known; however, women were not allowed citizenship status and likely were not eligible for funds.) The "care" response provided to those with extreme physical anomalies was exposure to the elements and death. Thus, as far back as ancient civilizations, variations of the human condition were identified in

TABLE 2.1	CONTEXTUAL FACTORS IN ANCIENT GREECE
Context	**Contextual Factors**
Dominant social values	Emphasis on beauty, perfection of form, loyalty to the state, hard work for the benefit of Greece
Geographic/natural	Southern Europe isolated from surrounding area by mountains; maritime travel still primitive
Economic	Agricultural sufficiency supported city dwellers; trade routes established across the Mediterranean
Political	Greek world organized into city-states; highly effective fighting techniques established them as leaders in war; earliest democracies provided one vote/one man for all citizens of the state (male landowners); social organization promoted through rhetorical public debate
Religious	Polytheism; knowledge of the gods transmitted through story; divination
Intellectual	Organization of knowledge by Aristotle; development and standardization of education; medical studies by Hippocrates; spiritual and supernatural hegemony

contrast to what was typical, and some explanations for extreme variation were met with legitimate acceptance and supportive responses, while others were not tolerated (Braddock & Parish, 2001).

Of particular note are two interactive influences on legitimacy criteria: the limited development of scientific theory coupled with the strong spirituality of ancient Greece (Stiker, 2000). Table 2.1 identifies the values and contextual factors of ancient Greece that were important in shaping views of what was typical and atypical; how those activities, appearances, and experiences were explained; and what values legitimated who was considered human, subhuman, and/or superhuman.

In the historical literature on early Jewish civilizations, atypical activity is not frequently discussed. The minimal references to appearance and daily activity that were considered flawed reveal that the nature of one's role in the community was in large part what determined what was typical and expected activity. Of particular relevance to this discussion is the prohibition of those who were "blemished" from the Jewish priesthood because of spiritual beliefs that priests were the direct link between God and the earth. However, congregation members did not carry those same expectations, and those with atypical appearance were permitted to be full participants in spiritual activity. Even with the permission to worship, those who were atypical in Jewish communities were in large part viewed as punished by God. The explanation for atypical appearance and activity was therefore spiritual and morally reprehensible. Yet the obligation for community care of such individuals was asserted (Abrams, 1998). Why some cultures met negative legitimacy determinations with care responses while others did not is a curious question that warrants further inquiry.

THE MIDDLE AGES

In the Middle Ages, it is interesting to note that the "typical" included human activity consistent with many activities, appearances, and experiences that today are classified as anomalous. According to historical researchers, so many individuals lived in poverty and squalor that they constituted the rule rather than the exception (Braddock & Parish, 2001; Langer, Geanakaplos, Hexter, & Pipes, 1975). Thus, their experience, appearance, and activity, resulting from exposure to severe living conditions, were not considered out of the ordinary. Illness and limitations in mobility and sensation (blindness, deafness, and so forth) were not at all unusual in poor communities. Further, given the limited knowledge about disease and nutrition, even the wealthy had experiences that are considered preventable today. In order to be atypical, one had to be extreme (Braddock & Parish, 2001).

Scholars have noted the existence of various competing explanations for extreme visible atypical activity. Among them were both spiritual attributions and demonic causes (Braddock & Parish, 2001). However, some accounts also reveal the emerging, albeit miniscule, role of scientific explanations demonstrated by the distinction between the treatable and the untreatable sick (Braddock & Parish, 2001). The small likelihood of survival for those who were unable to thrive at birth eliminated consideration of birth-based atypical activity from the literature or history of medieval times.

Individuals who behaved, communicated, or expressed thoughts differently from others were regarded as evil or as demons (Winzer, 1997). This religious explanation for activity that today is classified as mental illness was not surprising, given the Catholic Church's dominance in the Western world at the time. However, simplicity in cognitive activity that today would be regarded as mental retardation was sometimes explained as the possession of divine inspiration or a blessing given by God and depicted as such even in the artwork of the times (Levitas & Reid, 2003).

It is interesting to note that during the Middle Ages, explanations of atypical activity as socially and morally purposive began to emerge. Christian clergy suggested that individuals who exhibited atypical appearance and observable activity, even though immoral and monstrous, were created for the purpose of providing an opportunity for laypersons to exhibit tolerance and charitable behavior (Braddock & Parish, 2001). Thus, the roots of paternalism toward disabled individuals as objects of charity, whether or not they wanted it, can be seen as far back as the Middle Ages.

Because of the variety of explanations for the occurrences of extreme difference in activity, appearance, and experience, treatment and community responses were variable. Of particular note was the growth of institutional and charity approaches to individuals who were atypical. The beginning of faith-based hospitals was seated in the Middle Ages, as it was not unusual to find members of the clergy providing medical treatment to those who were considered ill. The role of faith in healing also has its roots in the Middle Ages. People who could not see or think as most others did, among other human differences, were often the objects of faith healing, a practice that provided concrete evidence of God's love, presence, and power (Stiker, 2000). Charity in the form of service and almsgiving exonerated the giver in the eyes of God, once again providing a purposive explanation for the extremes of human difference. Through the work of St. Francis of Assisi, the suffering of the poor and sick (particularly lepers) glorified the recipients of care as well as those providing care.

Braddock and Parish (2001) refer to evidence of some town support for people with atypical thinking and other forms of activity. However, because of the extreme poverty of the population at large, families would not have been able to provide long-term support, and so atypical individuals ultimately turned to begging for survival. This phenomenon is reflected in the artwork of the times, in which beggars are often depicted as individuals who are blind and lame (Braddock & Parish, 2001).

Not all differences were met with charity, however. In areas where the population believed in demonic explanations, those who behaved in ways that were described as "mad" were feared and persecuted as witches. Increasing social disorder in part was attributed to such individuals, and their murders therefore served as a rallying point for the masses (Stiker, 2000).

In summary, the Middle Ages brought important changes in the way that atypical human activity, appearance, and experience were conceptualized, explained, and treated. Because of the hegemony of the Catholic Church, purposive religious and moral explanations for human anomaly were advanced. Faith-based institutions were created to segregate "unusual individuals" from the public; to protect, treat, and care for them; and to transform their assumed plight into a venue for charity. Table 2.2 presents the values and contextual factors of the Middle Ages that were important in shaping views of what was typical and atypical; how those activities, appearances, and experiences were explained; and what values legitimated who was considered human, subhuman, and/or superhuman.

TABLE 2.2   CONTEXTUAL FACTORS IN THE MIDDLE AGES

Context	Contextual Factors
Dominant social values	Catholicism, charity, homogeneity
Geographic/natural	Black Plague killed nearly half the population in Europe and England in the mid-1300s
Economic	The population initially engaged primarily in rural farming through feudalistic arrangement; labor shortages pressured wages upward; monetary system developed; urban centers developed; technological advances improved agricultural production
Political	Manorial lords held power over serfs through landownership in exchange for military service; Catholic Church sponsored the Crusades; professional guilds controlled membership and production standards as towns developed
Religious	Primacy of Catholicism throughout Europe and England initially, challenged by Luther and Calvin in the 1500s; waning power of the Catholic Church, especially in England, resulted in the Reformation, a time of persecution for Protestants and other heretics
Intellectual	Intellectual advances were primarily in the area of religion, as reconciliation was attempted between the existence of hardship, mishap, and monstrosity on the one hand and belief in an all-knowing, loving God on the other

THE ENLIGHTENMENT

As the belief in demonology was slowly being challenged by science at the end of the Middle Ages, views of difference were being drastically altered. Advances in knowledge about the anatomy and physiology of the human body contributed to a growing sense that illness and differences in human activity could be explained by what could be observed in the physical world (Stiker, 2000). These views are reflected in the literature and art of the Renaissance period (Braddock & Parish, 2001). For example, Francis Bacon was particularly important in advancing the systematic study of these observable phenomena. In 1605, he published *The Advancement of Learning, Divine and Human,* in which he refuted the notion of moral punishment as the cause for behavior that was considered "mad." Humanism in art, emphasizing actual knowledge of underlying physical form, also emerged at this time, depicting detailed and accurate representations of the human body (Braddock & Parish, 2001).

This is not to say that moral explanations of difference in human activity, appearance, and experience ever disappeared as philosophers, clergy, and others continued to debate the relationship between God and nature (Durant, 1991). Questions about the purposive or serendipitous nature of anomaly were addressed, and many of the competing explanations that were posited remain operative and influential even today.

Explanations for the distinction between birth-based and acquired human atypicalities were developed during this time (Stiker, 2000) and served as platforms for value distinctions as well. For example, birth-based failures in activities necessary for typical growth were explained as "monstrosity," while differences in what individuals did that resulted from observable explanations such as injury were regarded as natural (Stiker, 2000). Distinctions were also drawn between activity, appearance, and experience that were consistent with what today would be referred to as mental illness and mental retardation (Braddock & Parish, 2001).

As in early civilizations, the legitimacy response to people who behaved in atypical ways was in large part influenced by how these behaviors were explained and how the explanations were valued. Moving forward in the Enlightenment era, however, brought increasingly complex explanations for all human activity, appearance, and experience, including the atypical. As religious hegemony gave way to philosophical and systematic intellectual dominance (Braddock & Parish, 2001), the interplay of economics and social factors in influencing analysis of all human experience emerged and influenced explanations of atypicality as well.

For example, the population of the poor often contained a disproportionate number of individuals who exhibited atypical activity and appearance. As evidenced by the English Poor Laws, social explanations for these differences were met with resources, while explanation seated in individual blame was not (Braddock & Parish, 2001). Even with the assertion of objectivity (Durant, 1991), the social bias toward self discipline was therefore apparent in legitimacy responses early in the history of Western civilization.

Those who were not blamed for their unusual behavior, appearance, and experience or who were not seen as dangers were often supported in communities (Braddock & Parish, 2001). Thus, looking through the lens of Explanatory Legitimacy Theory, we can see that the judgment of the explanation, not the descriptive element of human experience, was the determining factor in legitimating community response. Those who were perceived as out of the ordinary were treated differently, depending on how the community viewed the worth of the reasons for and results of their differences.

Not unlike current times, those with resources were not necessarily governed by the legitimacy criteria that shaped the response to poor individuals. Medical treatments for atypicality with medical explanations did exist and were available to those who could pay (Stiker, 2000). Although it is likely that economic status had always played a role in judgment and response, prior to the Enlightenment, the primacy of religion in shaping values and legitimate responses obfuscated or overshadowed other influences. In the Enlightenment, the recession of religion as explanatory for natural phenomena and the emerging emphasis on systematic production made it possible to view the important role of economic status in creating different legitimacy criteria for the poor and the rich (Braddock & Parish, 2001).

Institutions for people who behaved in ways that were observed and classified as mad (mental illness) proliferated during the 17th century. These served to remove unusual behaviors from public view rather than as a means to change behavior. Moreover, the manner in which people were treated in institutions was extremely harsh (Stiker, 2000), clearly indicating the devaluation of institutional residents.

In colonial America, explanations for frailty that were based in illness and aging were valued as worthy of care. Thus, in small communities with no other resources, the care of frail elders was provided by families. The ethnic, cultural, and religious homogeneity of the times fostered acceptance of poor, ill, and elderly members, who were not seen as blameworthy (Axinn & Stern, 2000). Further, atypical activity, appearance, and experience that were explained by poverty were not always distinguished from those explained by illness, and so informal arrangements for the care of the poor were not necessarily different from those provided to individuals whose atypicalities were explained by illness (see Table 2.3). This phenomenon is not surprising, given the infancy of medical thinking about human activity.

TABLE 2.3   CONTEXTUAL FACTORS IN THE ENLIGHTENMENT ERA

Context	Contextual Factors
Dominant social values	Poor distinguished as "worthy" or "unworthy"; in America, small communities that were ethnically, culturally, and religiously homogeneous cared for their own poor
Geographic/natural	Expansion of Western civilization to "the New World"
Economic	Beginning of industrialization: mass production and cost minimization; science of economics began; businesses of printing and journalism develop; banks established; profit motive developed
Political	Money is equated with power; English Poor Law of 1601 legislated financial relief in the community, especially for workhouses
Religious	America: homogeneous Puritanism
Intellectual	Rationalism; Bacon publishes *The Advancement of Learning, Divine and Human* in 1605 and refutes sin as the cause of mental illness; systematic thought extended to economics and society; literacy level increases

THE VICTORIAN ERA

Proceeding into the Victorian era, values of continental Europe, England, and the newly colonized America began to take divergent courses, as did conceptualization and legitimate judgment and response to the atypical. We therefore restrict our discussion here to the United States. The globalization paradigms that are emerging as New Social Theory and that reunite thinking about the world in a more integrated manner (Jameson & Miyoshi, 2001) are addressed later in this chapter in our discussion on the late 20th and early 21st centuries.

The rapid growth of America was a function of the intersection of many phenomena. Which influences were dominant over others is an ongoing debate among scholars and researchers and depends on their theoretical lenses. We therefore do not claim this history as absolute but offer it as a foundation on which to build.

The growth of the American economy had its roots in large part in the uninvited procurement of land on which American Indians lived and on the importation of slave and immigrant labor from other countries (Axinn & Stern, 2000; Holstein & Cole, 1996). However, the growth was not without unanticipated consequences. The existing system of poor relief in colonial America that was based in communal values and shared beliefs was ultimately challenged by the influx of people from diverse geographic regions of the world and by indigenous people. Thus, we begin to see the emergence of economic advantage coupled with social upheaval related to the juxtaposition of diverse cultural and ethnic groups (Goldberg, 1994). Given the increasing diversity among American communities, even before the concept of "normalcy" was formally articulated, what was atypical was defined in contrast to that which was known as common and acceptable in homogeneous communities (Davis, 1995).

Along with the increase of diverse inherent human characteristics such as race and ethnicity, explanations for what people did and did not do, how people looked, and what they experienced expanded as well with the burgeoning field of medicine. Note that medicine and scientific authority are major themes in disability conceptualization and history (Starr, 1982). We return to this important issue later in this chapter.

Despite the appearance of medicine, morality and social circumstance were still dominant explanations for unusual behavior, experience, and appearance. Moreover, with the vast resources available to "everyman" in the New World, tolerance (and thus acceptance of poverty as a legitimate explanation for the atypical) and charitable responses quickly degenerated. Poverty was assumed to be a self-imposed condition resulting from intrinsic laziness in an environment that was rich and in which economic productivity was becoming a paramount value (Axinn & Stern, 2000).

In response to the increasing social costs and disapproval of poverty, the towns and cities began to build poorhouses for the poor of all ages, the sick, and those behaving in a manner consistent with what today would be categorized as intellectually impaired, mentally ill, or socially deviant (Holstein & Cole, 1996). These categories of people held dependence and lack of productivity in common. Circumstances within the poorhouse were particularly and intentionally harsh to encourage families to support their members at all costs rather than abandon them to the care and thus the expense of the local government. The elderly were increasingly represented among the population in poorhouses as attitudes toward the unproductive frailty of old age grew increasingly unfavorable and illegitimate for sound community response (Holstein & Cole, 1996). Those who aged well were considered morally "worthy," and those who did not were "unworthy" of comfort and support.

As noted by Holstein and Cole (1996), the life of an immigrant was not often conducive to aging well, and thus emergent categories of legitimate worthiness were in large part a function of poverty of racial and ethnic groups. Thus, explanations of human activity, appearance, and experience increased in their complexity as people from diverse worlds became neighbors. While poverty, illness, and morality had been the primary explanations until now, observable diversity categories, including race, ethnicity, and other intrinsic human differences, were all thrown into the "explanation stew" without the public recognition that poverty and economic circumstance of these groups were underlying factors in explaining atypicality. Not unexpectedly, the legitimacy of explanations for human description was as diverse as the explanations themselves, given the multiple observable diversity groups with different and even competing values (Jost & Major, 2002).

 However, of particular importance in understanding disability and its treatment today is the development of the mathematical notion of "the norm" or "normal." As discussed by Davis (1995), the invention of mathematical statistics and concepts of central tendency resulted in the application of numbers to the description of all arenas of human activity, appearance, and experience. The French statistician Quetlet formulated the concept of "the normal man," who was both physically and morally normal. Based on probability, the concept of normal translates into the most frequently occurring phenomena. As shown in Figure 2.1, the highest part of the "normal curve" is also the average and contains the most frequently occurring scores. Extremes are the "abnormal" and appear on both ends of the curve as minimally occurring. Thus, common and frequent phenomena formed the basis for what we consider normal and are the foundation of many theories and practices today regarding the acceptable limits of human description.

Moreover, once observations of human phenomena were measured and categorized, the imperative that one "should" be normal (i.e., fall within the

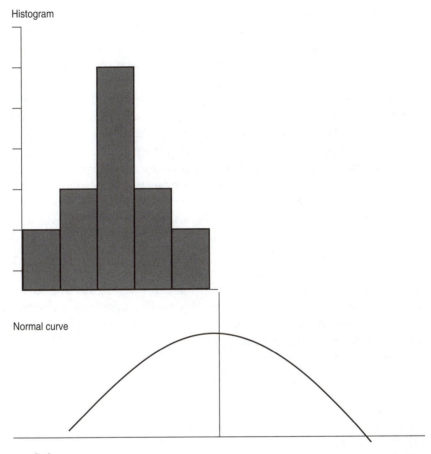

Figure **2.1**

most frequent range) was born. Observation therefore turned to prescription, and anyone exhibiting difference in activity, appearance, and/or experience was considered abnormal. The legitimacy of explanations for divergence from "what should be" determined valuation and treatment.

What sense do we make of all this? Consider the hallmark of the industrial era: mass production. Mechanization and production standards were based on statistical projections of what an average worker should "normally" accomplish within a given set of parameters, at minimum. Efficiency experts, such as Fredrick Taylor (Kanigel, 1999), aimed to study and increase the rate of normal production as a basis for economic growth.

As industrialization advanced and associated economic productivity with legitimate goodness, links between standardized expectations, moral judgment, unemployment, and disproportionate poverty among people with activity, appearance, and/or experiential differences further located legitimacy of explanations in terms of productivity. The attribution of nonnormal activity, appearance, and experience to assumed productivity limitation was and remains an important determination of legitimacy. For example, unusual body shapes or motor activity were expected to result in slower rates of production; thus, those individuals who exhibited these anomalies by virtue of appearance were automatically assumed to be of less economic value than their "normal counterparts."

Legitimate support responses to abnormal individuals, as expected, followed value judgments about who was worthy and who was not. Poverty in and of itself was no longer considered a legitimate explanation for atypical activity or need, and thus the poor were not treated well (Axinn & Stern, 2000; Stone, 1986). Those who could not compete were unable to find jobs to generate income and thus fell into the ranks of the morally reprehensible to be met with the legitimate response of incarceration in poorhouses. What made people legitimately good was the capacity to earn (Longmore & Umansky, 2001; Schriner & Scotch, 1998). As presented in Table 2.4, complexity of contextual factors increased during the Victorian era, setting the stage for the dominance of economic resources in shaping notions of typicality, explanations for atypicality, the criteria for legitimately acceptable explanations, and legitimate rationale for community response.

TABLE 2.4   CONTEXTUAL FACTORS IN THE VICTORIAN ERA

Context	Contextual Factors
Dominant social values	Increasing diversity in ethnicity, values, and customs across the population; productivity; profit
Geographic/natural	Immigration from diverse parts of the world
Economic	Industrialization; economic expansion across the country using slave labor; global markets available even for produce after the development of steamships and refrigeration
Political	Democracy with two-party system
Religious	Mainly Christian, but diverse across slave and Asian populations
Intellectual	Quetlet (invention of statistics and the concept of normative thinking); Locke (ideas are not innate); Hume (knowledge depends on a series of perceptions); behaviors are based in "habits" of thinking; utilitarianism (virtue is the greatest good for the greatest number of people)

Table 2.5 provides a summary of the historical trends that we have discussed so far in this chapter. Look closely at it before moving into the discussion of the 20th century. A view through the lens of Explanatory Legitimacy Theory reveals the role of contextual factors—including but not limited to economics, diversity of origin, geography, and intellectual trends—in shaping values that distinguish typical and atypical, that provide explanations for both, and that determine the worth of individuals and groups. As discussed earlier, before the 20th century and in light of the hegemony of spiritual attributions for human phenomena, atypicality was explained primarily as supernatural, moral, or not human. As intellectual development advanced scientific understanding and informed and placed economic production as primary, the turn of the century introduced new factors that significantly changed these explanations of atypical activity, appearance, and experience and the legitimacy determinations about the worth of individuals and their treatment.

THE EARLY 20TH CENTURY

Thus far, we have refrained from using the term "disability" to describe the characteristic that locates individuals among those with atypical activity due to medical explanations. The use of the term "disability" is relatively new and remains vague. Before "disability" was used to describe a group of people with permanent medical-diagnostic explanations that affected their daily activity, appearance, and/or experience in atypical ways, words such as "cripple," "blind," "deaf," and "handicap" were often used. In an effort to create a publicly respectful and politically correct language to refer to the undesirable atypicality explained by medical-diagnostic conditions, the term "disability" is now used most widely supported especially by nondisabled individuals (Heumann, 1993). Although the term "disability" was not primary until the 1980s, we can add this term to our history now, as it is relevant to the time period we are discussing.

The early 1900s saw disability as a personal attribute (Linton, 1998). An individual who exhibited atypicality in the sensory, physical, psychological, and/or cognitive arenas and who had a bona fide long-term or permanent medical-diagnostic explanation for that activity was considered legitimately handicapped. Thus, while there were many other explanations for atypicality, such as poverty and cultural difference, atypical activity, appearance, or experience due to medical condition became the foundation of the classification of disability and thus the object of legitimate active and palliative response by medical and related fields (Hahn, 1993; Oliver, 1996b).

TABLE 2.5   GENERAL HISTORICAL TRENDS

Historical Period	Atypical Activity/ Appearance/ Experience	Explanation	Legitimacy Worth	Treatment
Ancient Greece	Deformed infant	None	Not human	Left to die
	Not seeing, not hearing, lameness	Caused by the gods for sinful acts, either by the afflicted individual or by an ancestor	Immoral	Ostracized
	Not seeing, not hearing, lameness	War injury	Well respected	Given special care and pension
	Activity consistent with what today is known as mental illness	Supernatural	Well respected	Participated in community life
Early Jewish civilizations	Blemished appearance	Spiritual and moral	Not worthy enough for priesthood	Participated in community life
Medieval times	Individuals who behaved, communicated, or expressed thoughts differently from others	Spiritual	Evil or demonic	Persecuted
	Atypical appearance and physical activity	Were placed on earth to engender charity and tolerance from the masses	Evil or demonic	Cared for by clergy
	Simplicity in cognitive activity that today would be regarded as mental retardation	Spiritual	Divine	Participated in community life
Enlightenment era	Individuals who behaved, communicated, or expressed thoughts differently from others	Wrong assemblage of right ideas	Feared and degraded	Received harsh treatment in institutions
	Atypical appearance and physical activity present at birth	Monstrosity	Disgust	Harsh life in poorhouses
	Atypical appearance and physical activity acquired after birth	Natural causes	Respected	Participated in community life
	Simplicity in cognitive activity that today would be regarded as mental retardation	Wrong ideas	Accepted, not respected	Participated in community life

(Continued)

TABLE
2.5   (Continued)

HIstorical Period	Atypical Activity/ Appearance/ Experience	Explanation	Legitimacy Worth	Treatment
Victorian era	Poor frail elderly	Personal weakness	Scorned	Segregated in poorhouses
	Poverty, sickness	Personal weakness related to gender, ethnicity, or race	Derided	Segregated in poorhouses
	Atypical physical activity and appearance evident from birth	Abnormal, morally inferior	Disgust	Segregated in institutions
	Atypical physical activity and appearance acquired after birth	Abnormal, morally inferior	Respected if injured in war or able to work	Participated in community life, especially if able to work
	Individuals who behaved, communicated, or expressed thoughts differently from others	Abnormal, morally inferior	Not respected	Received humane treatment in institutions

Because of the hegemony of medical explanations for atypical activity, appearance, and experience as definitional of "disability," medical conditions themselves and the distinctions among them became synonyms for disability types as well as the focus of legitimate value and worth determinations. For example, legislation and medical and professional specialties often speak to labels such as "cognitive disability," "psychiatric disability," "physical disability," and so forth. These diagnostic delineations were and remain the basis for service systems for disabled people.

Similar to previous historical eras, individuals who sustained war injuries resulting in permanent medical conditions that were considered the cause of atypicality were considered most worthy of benefits, while those who were believed to have control over their medical conditions, despite the severity and impact on activity, appearance, and/or experience, were not (Pfeiffer, 2002).

Of particular note was the clear value division between mental and physical medical-diagnostic explanations. While most atypicality was and is considered undesirable, those with psychiatric and cognitive explanations for their performance, appearance, and experience differences were clearly considered and thus treated as legitimately inferior to those who had acceptable physical diagnostic explanations. These value differences were important determinants in shaping legitimate differential care responses within the multiple systems of care, as discussed next (Davis, 1995).

For example, the institutionalization of people whose atypicalities were attributed to mental illness diagnoses illustrates the limited value placed on this category of diagnostic explanation. The creation of specialized institutions for people with mental illness explanations for atypicality was accelerated in large part because of the efforts of Dorothea Dix and her cohorts during the 1840s. Dix traveled the United States documenting and publicizing the horrific circumstances of people with mental illness and lobbying for treatment (Gleeson, 1997).

Concurrent with the effort of Dix and others with analogous agendas, the belief that mental illness was a curable medical condition was an important influence on the proliferation of and treatment provided in large mental institutions. However, almost immediately these institutions became overcrowded, and goals for treatment cure were replaced by less expensive custodial care at best. The very limited placement of institutional patients in community homes occurred during this time not as a means to promote community living but as an economic response to overcrowding.

Similarly, institutions for people with intellectual impairment explanations for atypicality both grew in number and became overcrowded (Holstein & Cole, 1996). Initially intended as training sites designed to return productive citizens to the community, these institutions also responded to economic influences by resorting to custodial care that was concerned primarily with the management of inpatient populations. Discharge of people with intellectual impairment explanations for atypicality back into the community was complicated by negative social attitudinal responses toward intellectual impairment as well as limitations in family supports and work opportunities (Braddock & Parish, 2001).

Note that although institutional treatment expanded, the majority of people with atypicality explained by intellectual impairment diagnoses remained with families in the community. However, institutions proliferated for several reasons. First, diagnostic explanations made prediction of lifelong atypicality possible. Second, care provided by family members, usually women, competed with remunerative work or care of typical children. Perhaps most important, institutional responses were the locus of a new industry (Gill, 1992), which we refer to as the care industry. Many professionals and nonprofessionals alike gained significant economic benefit from their work with institutionalized atypical individuals (Gill, 1992).

Dissimilar to those with mental and cognitive explanations for atypicality, treatment of individuals with diagnostic explanations for physical impairment was rehabilitative and increased rapidly during the early 20th century within the rubric of charity. Illustrating the approach that individuals with legitimate explanations for atypicality were objects of charity, organizations and agencies, such as the National Society for Crippled Children and Adults in 1907 (later the Easter Seals), were established. Different from the charitable path for worthy but nonemployable atypical individuals, the value on work and production was reflected in public policy and legislation as early as 1902 in the form of state workers' compensation laws. The importance of economic productivity in shaping care responses to atypicality was well embedded in formal and informal legitimacy responses by this time. For example, in 1920, the U.S. Congress passed the first civilian vocational rehabilitation law in the country, following the creation of rehabilitation services for veterans of World War I (Braddock & Parish, 2001).

Directed mainly at persons injured at work, the services also covered those who sustained injuries, illness, or who had congenital conditions that were explained by observable "physical abnormalities." Of course, any attribution of blame or self-imposed atypicality was not an acceptable explanation for legitimate rehabilitation response (Obermann, as cited in Braddock & Parish, 2001, p. 42). The primary expected outcome of rehabilitation for "physically impaired" workers and worthy others was a return to productive employment.

It is important to note that regardless of the atypicality, in the early and even middle part of the 20th century, explanations were primarily medical, located within an individual's body, and thus were both the individual's misfortune and the individual's responsibility. It followed that the care or cure responses were seen as "helping" atypical individuals to improve or as providing a place for them to exist where they would not burden communities and interfere in the economy.

The division between public and charitable supports and services was clearly an economic function. Those whose work-sustained explanations for atypicality or those who could be restored to employment were considered legitimately worthy of public support, while those with illegitimate explanations were seen as objects of charity. This division implicitly or explicitly reflects legitimacy determinations and has been essential in shaping disability as an economic commodity in the 20th and 21st centuries.

SUMMARY

In this chapter, we have used Explanatory Legitimacy Theory as the analytic lens through which we traced the history of the typical and atypical, explanations for diverse human descriptors, and context-embedded values and beliefs that shaped determinations of human goodness and community response to atypicality. As shown in this chapter, the three elements of our approach to disability (description, explanation, and legitimacy)—were clearly visible in all historical accounts. Not only have notions of atypicality and explanations changed, but the parameters for legitimate worth and entitlement to response resources have shifted in response to contextual, natural, chronological, spiritual, and intellectual trends. Nevertheless, morality and intrinsic character are still important considerations in how the atypical is viewed, explained, and perceived as acceptable or not. In the 20th and 21st centuries, the emergence of three factors—economic productivity (which we discuss as capitalism in Chapter 5); medical knowledge, technology, and professional authority; and diversity—have had and continue to have significant roles in definitions of typicality and atypicality, how atypicality is explained, and the differential determination of these explanations as legitimate disability status and response.

DISABILITY IN THE 20TH AND 21ST CENTURIES

In Chapter 2, we looked back at the history of disability in Western civilizations. As the chronology unfolded, the role of values in judging the acceptability and worthiness of explanations for human activity, appearance, and experience were highlighted as the primary influence on categorization and response. In this chapter, we examine disability in contemporary times through the lens of Explanatory Legitimacy Theory. What we learn through this stance is that the influence of contextual factors on value judgments (not on human activity, appearance, or experience or even the explanations attributed to human phenomena) is the key to understanding categorization, the legitimacy of individuals and groups who fit within a category, and the responses that are deemed legitimate for members.

Because there are so many conceptualizations of disability, its contemporary history, and its current meaning, we may not include the full scope of literature in this analysis specifically. However, as we indicated, our work builds on previous literature, research, and theory, and we therefore attempt to capture the breadth of current thinking that informs our stance and our conclusions.

We begin this chapter where we left off in our look back in time at the turn of the 20th century by suggesting that contemporary definitions of and responses to disability are shaped by the three primary contextual factors: (a) medical science, technology, and professional authority; (b) industrialization and the advancing primacy of capitalism; and (c) human diversity. We turn to a discussion of each of these now.

MEDICAL SCIENCE, TECHNOLOGY, AND PROFESSIONAL AUTHORITY

The advancement of medical science and technology has been a crucial factor in reshaping conceptualizations of disability and responses to it. As we saw in the last chapter, Enlightenment thinking provided the foundation for the growth of medical science and for the emergence of medical explanations for atypicality in the mid-19th century. However, advancing professionalization of medicine, not the scientific knowledge itself, was the element that positioned physicians as the dominant group in shaping definitions of disability (Kane, Kane, & Ladd, 1998; Starr, 1984). Thus, because physicians were able to assert professional authority, atypicality became, and to a large extent remains, synonymous with long-term and/or medical conditions.

The increasing sophistication in knowledge and technology not only shaped disability as primarily medical but also set the medical and health professions as guardians and gatekeepers in the lives of people with legitimate diagnoses. We provide additional detail on this important point later in the chapter when we examine the important role that medical and health professionals play in how disability legislation has been formulated and enacted (Gleeson, 1997).

Pharmaceutical development, diagnostic, and treatment techniques and technological advancement not only have made it possible for people to survive illness but also have significantly extended the life span of the typical adult. Advancing technology and scientific knowledge created the foundation for the development of professional education as well as the need for expertise. Those who completed extended education were therefore assured a high standard of knowledge acquisition and use, and the scene was set for restrictive licensure designed to maintain the knowledge in the hands of a few experts on whom those who did not possess it became dependent (Starr, 1982). This dependency, in a context of capitalist dominance, provided an excellent opportunity for economic advantage exercised by health professionals, physicians in particular, who were held in high esteem and paid handsomely (Friedson, 1980). So as we can see that the advancement of scientific knowledge and technology was important in lifesaving and enhancing strategies as well as in the creation of an elite group of professionals who exchanged specialized knowledge and skill for status and economic benefit.

As the 20th century unfolded, the explosion in science, coupled with the desirability of health professional status, was influential in the proliferation of specializations within medicine and in the development of health professions, including medicine, that both named and crafted responses to individuals and groups with disabilities (Friedson, 1980). Included among these fields were nursing, psychology, social work, and the rehabilitation professions (e.g., physical therapy, occupational therapy, speech and language pathology, and vocational rehabilitation).

It is interesting to note that as these professions grew and became competitive, the team approach over other possible collaboration strategies was selected and espoused as the best method for determining and responding to disability. In this framework, professionals theoretically pool their expertise to make decisions about how best to work with, treat, or assist disabled individuals and groups. Many models of teamwork have been posited (O'Brien & O'Brien, 1997), all based on communication and the assumption that mutually exclusive expertise will be combined to achieve the most desirable intervention results. However, the team approach, in which multiple professionals, sometimes with competitive value and ethical professional codes, each charge for service, has provided the opportunity and justification for another layer of intervention: managed care (Kane et al., 1998). Under managed care and similar approaches, individuals with disabilities who receive services from multiple providers are assigned to an individual who orchestrates both services and payment for those services.

Thus, while technology, professional knowledge, and social status have brought major opportunity for providers, these factors have also created limiting conditions in that the increasing cost of technology has elicited managed care control and has forced providers from small practices into large global corporations that can purchase and maintain costly technologically based research and practice (Stone, 2002).

CAPITALISM

There are few who would dispute that capitalism is a critical factor in how disability has been conceptualized, defined, and treated in the 20th and 21st centuries. On many levels, capitalism, productivity, and profit have been primary in shaping our current views of legitimate disability and our responses to these views.

Three points related to capitalism are important in our discussion in this chapter. First, poverty and illness, although not seen as distinct in the 18th and early 19th centuries, were clearly separated in their conceptualization and treatment in the 20th (Braddock & Parrish, 2001; Holstein & Cole, 1996). Poverty as an explanation for atypicality was no longer a legitimate rationale for membership in a categorical group that was worthy of any more than a subsistence response despite the recognition that poverty has negative consequences for all domains of human activity, appearance, and experience (Axinn & Stern, 2000). Only in the latter part of the 20th century did the relationship between poverty and disability once again become the object of attention and response. The roles of poor living conditions and limited access to health care have been increasingly recognized and attended to in the literature and in some respects in legislation and public response. Among many medical diagnostic disability groups, poverty remains disproportionately high as both causative and consequential, rendering the distinction between poverty and medical diagnosis as explanatory for atypicality difficult to make (Harris & Associates, 1986, 1998). We look at the reasons for this phenomenon later in this chapter.

A related issue is the role of work potential in defining and responding to disability. If an individual was unable to work, the burden on family members was recognized and addressed differently, depending on the nature of the medical diagnostic explanation for atypicality and other demographic and personal variables that shaped family and community response to burden.

For example, early small private nursing homes that provided safety and care for disabled family members were typically operated by women caring for their husbands and one or two other people until such homes were replaced with larger institutions with an increasing concern for profit (Dunlop, cited in Holstein & Cole, 1996). Note here the gender role in caregiving. Although not extensively explored and addressed in research and analysis until the women's liberation movement and a shift in gender equity, gender was a critical factor both in culturally and in economically influencing who legitimately could receive care, by whom, and of what nature (Stone, 2002). Because traditional gender roles did not position women in remunerative employment, they were default caregivers and were vulnerable to limited care if no other women were available to provide it (Kane et al., 1998).

Similarly, in institutions for those with mental and intellectual explanations for atypicality, capitalism was integral in shaping policy and practices. Institutions isolated individuals from the community, removing the burden of care from those who were employable or who needed to care for nondisabled children. Furthermore, during the Great Depression, administrators developed operating strategies for employing patients as an unpaid workforce (Katz, 1996). These strategies, asserted to be therapeutic, perpetuated the economic survival and growth of institutional care in times of economic scarcity and set a precedent for the future economic exploitation of individuals with mental and cognitive diagnostic explanations for atypical activity, appearance, and/or experience (Braddock & Parrish, 2001). When institutional care was deemed as too costly, deinstitutionalization was initiated, with the rhetorical justification of community inclusion but with limited services and supports to assist individuals to successfully adjust to life in the community.

A second point regarding capitalism is the development of what we call the "disability industry." Numerous interest groups sought to derive significant economic benefit from direct and tangential involvement with disability. For example, regardless of how nursing homes were originally conceptualized, care systems grew into a multi-billion-dollar industry in which economic stake holding and profit were and continue to be driving forces (Gill, 1992; Gleeson, 1997). As we indicated earlier, increasing costs of technology and insurance also paved the way for the proliferation of global provider corporations whose focus is on maximizing profit.

Third, there is an increasing shift from the not-for-profit to the profit sector in many parts of the disability industry, highlighting the recognition on the part of disabled individuals and the industry that disability has the potential to

TABLE

3.1

Accessibility Design Resources
Articles, Books to Buy!, Companies

Computer Accessibility Products
Assistive Technology Programs, Augmentative Communication Devices, Books to Buy! . . .

Disability Related Products/Services
Adapted Special Needs Clothing, Assistive Devices/Products for Independent Living, Bed/Comfort Products . . .

Home Automation/Environmental Control
Companies, Information about Home Automation, Microphones . . .

Sports Training And Athletic Competition
Books, Equestrian/Horse Riding, and Organizations . . .

Travel and Recreation Resources
Air Travel, Books to Buy!, Destinations . . .

Wheelchair/Mobility Products
Abledata Fact sheets, All-Terrain Wheelchairs, Books to Buy! . . .

create new and important consumer markets. See Table 3.1 for several of the most recent Web sites that market to disabled consumers.

DIVERSITY

Before discussing the influence of diversity on values and practices relevant to disability, an important point of clarification is necessary. Originally, we developed Explanatory Legitimacy Theory to focus analysis and guide social action specific to disability. However, as we read and think about and then challenge ideas, we realize that Explanatory Legitimacy Theory and its foundations (Jost & Major, 2002) apply broadly to all categorical systems. Thus, for us, diversity categories such as ethnicity, race, and gender fall under similar analytic lenses to disability. As we challenge current categorization within disability, so too do we question and challenge other taxonomies that are used to categorize humanity. We therefore suggest that similar to our classification of human activity, appearance, and experience, diversity has two elements: diversity patina and diversity depth. Diversity patina refers to the observable dimensions of category creation and membership attribution. We chose the word "patina" to reflect our view that although diversity categorization at this level is made by the possession of discernable common characteristics shared by all members, each member retains unique marks as well. Diversity depth is the element of diversity that is unseen, unheard, and thus analogous to what we have termed "reportable." Only through inference is categorization made and membership attributed. Think, for example, of gender and sexual orientation. For the most part, gender is an example of diversity patina. Typically, we can discern if an individual is male or female but can only infer sexual orientation even when if the individual is behaving or appearing in a stereotypical gender role. Moreover, why some attributes have been selected as legitimate diversity categories (e.g., race, ethnicity, class, and gender) and others have not (e.g., body shape, activity preference, and activity talent) is another important pointof analysis to which Explanatory Legitimacy Theory needs to be applied. However, because of our focus on disability in this book, we limit our discussion of other diversity categories and address it only as it applies to disability.

At this point in our discussion of history, we mention diversity patina because observable differences in human appearance as a result of the new juxtaposition of ethnically, racially, and otherwise diverse groups resulting from immigration constituted a critical concern affecting disability legitimacy. Immigrant populations settled in many cities, and African Americans who had populated mainly the rural South began moving to urban centers to find work. The proximity of diverse groups, while idealized by some of the popular culture of the time, created friction and intolerance that played out in and affected the identification and care of those who exhibited atypicality due to legitimate medical explanations (Scotch, 2001). For example, in response to exclusion from agencies and services for Anglo-American whites, the African American community created its own self-help, hospitals, homes for the aged, unemployment relief, and other similar services based on the values of kinship and mutual aid. Similarly, ethnic groups outside the mainstream of observable Anglo-American categorization, such as Jews, created their own systems of aid and support (Abrams, 1998; Percy, 1989).

At this point in history, although it was always present in practice, an increasing awareness of the role of gender in legitimate response to disability determination was observable. Women, who were not usually in a position to formally assert disability membership for themselves and others (typically, they were not physicians), were responsible for the legitimate response, including the initiation, organization, and conduct of caregiving efforts (Holstein & Cole, 1996). This activity distinction, based on the diversity patina of gender, played out in professional status as well, with women dominating in subordinate fields to medicine, such as nursing and social work.

However, as the 20th century proceeded and the attention to diversity became both more complex and central to the public, defining and responding to disability has taken on diversity depth to some extent. An increasing focus on multiculturalism and cultural competency has been omnipotent in the literature and rhetoric, shifting the diversity stance beyond race, ethnicity, and culture to include human differences together with, but not limited to, age, sexual orientation, health and illness, and ability. The move on the part of disability rights activists to position disability within the multicultural/human diversity discourse and to define a distinct disability cultural diversity patina have both benefited and limited people with medical explanations for atypical activity, appearance, and/or experience (Gilson & DePoy, 2000). Benefits have included increasing recognition and protective legislation (Charlton, 1998). However, the lack of diversity depth has contributed to divisions among those with observable and reportable atypicality and to the exposure of disability patina to a multitude of negative attitudes and social practices based on the ascription of assumed incompetence to the presence of an observable atypicality (Bassnett, 2001).

Consider, for example, the diagnostic explanation of Down syndrome. The designation of Down syndrome as a legitimate medical explanation for atypicality has placed individuals with that label under protected status. Social action resulting from this status includes but is not limited to consent degrees forcing deinstitutionalization and supporting community inclusion. However, while civil rights have been asserted and progress has been made in this arena, individuals with Down syndrome as an explanation for atypicality continue to be subject to stigma and to exclusion from community life and its supports and services (Scotch, 2001). Consider the individual who is able to work in competitive employment but because of discrimination is not given a chance despite his or her skills.

The intersection of these three important historical trends has given rise to medicalized definitions of and policy and practice responses to individuals with atypicalities. As we will see, further events and influences were also operational in the paradigmatic shifts in stance that have taken place since the latter part of the 20th century. We now turn to a chronology of disability policy and legislation as reflection.

DISABILITY POLICY AND LEGISLATION IN THE 20TH CENTURY

Disability legislation in the 20th century falls into two primary categories: (a) legislation and policy to provide resources to legitimately disabled or needy persons and (b) civil rights legislation. In the early part of the century, the construct of civil rights was not relevant to disability legislation. As we will see, however, continued exclusion from participation in communities and in the economy shifted the stance of disability-related legislation into the realm of protection of rights.

As you read the narrative that follows, we would like to draw your attention to several important points that are illuminated by the application of

Explanatory Legitimacy Theory to public policy and law. First, both policy and legislation address explanation not description. Notice the values that inhere in the policy and legislation determining what explanations are acceptable to belong to the category of disability. Second, although not explicit, the nature of responses reveals the legitimacy of the explanation (Scotch, 2001; Scotch & Schriner, 1997).

Thus, those individuals and groups in which atypicality is explained by a valued rationale are afforded more benefits than others with analogous needs but less valued explanations. For example, individuals who exhibit atypicality as a result of a work injury are eligible for workers' compensation and related resources. These benefits are significantly greater than the subsistence benefits offered to individuals and groups who have never worked but whose atypicalities may be severely limiting to participation in communities and may even have been lifelong. We turn now to the legislation for a further example.

We begin our chronology with the first formal legislative effort to assist individuals whose atypicalities were explained by injury in service to the country. The 1918 Smith-Sears Veterans' Act established a vocational rehabilitation program for soldiers, most of whom were injured during World War I. As such, the first clear determination of being legitimately disabled was institutionalized in statute. Note here that the first legal disability legitimacy criterion was injury at war, illuminating the value that was attributed to war veterans.

The Smith-Fess Act of 1920, or the Civilian Vocational Rehabilitation Act, served to extend the designation of disability legitimacy by way of providing a 50% match to state rehabilitation programs for counseling, vocational training, and job placement for civilians with atypical physical activity explained by medical diagnosis. Both legislated programs sought to restore work activity in the lives of legitimately disabled individuals, revealing the value on work productivity both in the legitimacy criterion and in the legislated response to disability. Note that the observable nature of atypicality and the legitimate medical explanation were the targets of this legislation.

This federal vocational rehabilitation program was made permanent and further expanded with passage of the Social Security Act of 1935. The Depression and the fall into poverty of individuals who were previously considered productive earners expanded legitimate explanations for disability and the need for support at least through the 1980s, when conservative reform once again narrowed legitimacy determinations for benefits. Thus, legislative changes to the Social Security Act of 1935 not only enlarged the range of legitimate service responses, such as provisions for medical services and prosthetic devices, but also included benefits to the families of individuals with some atypicalities. The act gave funds and income supports to states to assist blind citizens, indigent dependent children, and elderly adults. However, the level of support for this program, in which poverty and disability were combined, was minimal. It is important to note, however, that the context of the Depression and unexpected poverty, considered to be beyond the control of individuals for so many groups who were previously valued and employed, changed the public and legislative stances to allow public responses to need explained by poverty.

Percy (1989) notes that blind individuals and their allies were the first of the categorical disability groups to organize and seek resources for their own benefit. The trend to establish categorical institutions that were delimited by sensory atypicality was founded in this initial political effort.

Highlighting the critical importance of capitalism and economics in defining disability and responses to it is the continuing focus of rehabilitation programs, as established under the Social Security Act, on assisting individuals to enter or reenter the workforce (Braddock, 2001; Percy, 1989). These federal vocational or work-focused programs were consistent with the state policies and programs initiated in the early 1900s for workers who were seriously injured on the job, primarily in manufacturing and industrial firms. It is interesting to note that while these occupational, or workers' compensation, programs were structured by state governments, they were funded by private insurance companies to provide medical benefits, vocational rehabilitation, income supports, and death benefits to workers injured or killed on the job. Thus, public responses provided profit for private enterprise.

Income supports for workers between the ages of 50 and 64 whose atypicalities were explained by injuries sustained on the job that were determined to be of "long, continued, and indefinite duration" (Percy, 1989, p. 46) were codified in federal statute by the 1956 amendments to the Social Security Act: Social Security Disability Insurance. On the basis of atypical activity explained by work injury, individuals aged 50 and over were eligible to receive benefits that would ordinarily not have been available until retirement age. However, these benefits were available only to those who had already been employed in jobs in which they contributed to Social Security. This legislation clearly demonstrates the value of work and of economic contribution to public coffers, as both had to be present in order for an injured individual to receive public resources. Further amendments to the Social Security Act subsequently provided an additional clarification to the legitimacy criterion of disability: "have lasted, or are expected to last, not less than twelve months" (Percy, 1989, p. 46). We therefore see the meaning and codification of "long-term medical explanation" for need in these legislative changes.

In 1972, the U.S. Congress created the Supplemental Security Income (SSI) program, authorizing income supports to individuals who were designated as "needy, aged, blind, . . . [or] disabled, regardless of geographic location" (Percy, 1989, p. 46). This program provided supports subject to an economic needs test. In including disability with poverty in federal legislation, the presence of poverty in the lives of disabled individuals was brought to public attention. Unfortunately, this legislation provided a disincentive for individuals qualifying as legitimately disabled to begin or return to work since many were not able to realize even the minimal benefits from employment that were afforded by SSI. Because SSI was decreased and/or terminated if remunerative income was received, many disabled individuals who faced discrimination or had limited work skills remained in poverty on the subsistence wages and benefits of SSI. Current legislative efforts have begun to remediate this work disincentive by allowing individuals to maintain SSI benefits, such as Medicaid health insurance, while being employed.

Thus far, we have been considering federal legislation and programs that have been work or economically focused. Moreover, the stance that values productivity and economic contribution can be clearly seen in how legislation was conceptualized and structured. Beginning in the 1960s—principally at the urging of parents—legislators and other federal government officials began to turn their attention to the educational needs of children. Amendments in 1966 to the Elementary and Secondary Education Act of 1965 authorized "funds to states to assist states in the initiation, expansion, and improvement of programs for the education of handicapped children" (Percy, 1989, p. 46). This legislation is important in marking a shift in stance and thus in legitimacy status and benefits. Legitimate explanations for the atypicality and thus eligibility for resources expanded to include school-age children with diagnostic cognitive, psychiatric, and physical explanations.

In 1968, with the passage of the Handicapped Children's Early Education Assistance Act, Congress once again changed the legitimacy criteria to include preschool-age children with bona fide diagnostic explanations. Note that these legislative acts provided resources to children who were enrolled in school and preschool, thereby extending responses to those groups who had never participated in the workforce but who were also considered as innocents (Asch, 2001) and not in control of the explanation for atypicality.

A landmark shift in stance from the provision of resources to the recognition of civil rights occurred in 1968 with the passage of the Architectural Barriers Act and then the Rehabilitation Act of 1973. Subsequent civil rights legislation includes the Education for All Handicapped Children Act (Public Law [P.L.] 94–142), first signed in 1975 and regularly modified (now the Individuals with Disabilities Education Act (P.L. 100–476); the Air Carrier Access Act of 1986 (P.L. 99–435, 100 Stat. 1080 [1987]); the Fair Housing Amendments Act of 1988 (P.L. 100–430, 102, Stat. 1619 [1988]); and most recently the Americans with Disabilities Act of 1990 (ADA) and the special provision for the protection of disabled women in the Violence Against Women's Act (2000).

The Architectural Barriers Act focused on the removal of physical barriers or architectural impediments to federally financed buildings. As originally conceived, this legislation sought to address issues and needs raised by individuals with atypical physical activity regardless of medical explanation. The Education for All Handicapped Children Act asserted the right for all children to public education in the least restricted environment.

While the ADA (P.L. 101–336, 104 Stat. 327 [1990]) can rightly be thought of as the primary civil rights act for individuals with atypicalities explained by legitimate medical conditions, it is difficult to appreciate the significance of the ADA without consideration of its "predecessor," the Rehabilitation Act of 1973. Prior to the passage of this act, disabled persons were not afforded protections against discrimination despite legislation that prohibited similar discriminatory practices on the basis of other diversity categories, including race, color, national origin, sex, and religion (Berkowitz, 1994). Representative Charles Vanik (D-Ohio) and Senator Hubert Humphrey (D-MN) considered amending Title VI of the Civil Rights Act of 1964 (P.L. 88–352, 78 Stat. 241 [1964]) that outlawed discrimination on the basis of category membership related to race, color, or national origin to include civil rights protection for members of the category of disability. However, this approach was rejected on the basis of concerns that broadening the civil rights legislation to include an undetermined number of category members might weaken or lessen the impact of the act for racial and ethnic minority categories (Berkowitz, 1994).

The tension among groups experiencing discrimination is clearly visible in the rationale to exclude disabled individuals from the same protections afforded to other legitimate minority categories. Thus, prior to 1973, individuals who were atypical because of medical conditions were not considered as legitimate for the protections offered by civil rights legislation. Therefore, the passage of the Rehabilitation Act of 1973 marked an important new stance: the recognition of legitimacy of medical explanations of disability for protection parallel to legislative practices that had been adopted on behalf of other minority categories. In areas where the federal government was involved directly or indirectly, the Rehabilitation Act of 1973 required that transportation, housing, education, and employment either were or had to be made accessible to members of the disabled category. All programs, agencies, organizations, and activities that received federal assistance were ordered to comply with the provisions of the act. Note here that implicit in this legislation is the legitimacy of some medical explanations—those that explain mobility and sensation atypicality and not others.

The legislation was also subject to the influence of economics regardless of its basis in codified moral correctness of the times. The Rehabilitation Act of 1972, which passed with relative ease in both the House and the Senate, was pocket vetoed by President Nixon on October 27, 1972, on the basis of a claim that, among other factors, the act was too costly. A nearly identical bill was introduced into Congress in 1973. President Nixon again vetoed it on March 27, 1973. On May 23, 1973, the bill was reintroduced, this time with less costly responses, such as limited funding and fewer programs. It was then signed into law by President Nixon on September 26, 1973 (Treanor, 1993).

The Rehabilitation Act had two focal responses. The first dealt primarily with an extension and elaboration of a variety of vocational rehabilitation laws beginning with the Vocational Education Act of 1917 (P.L. 63–347, 39 Stat. 929 [1917]). The secondary focus was the civil rights or antidiscrimination agenda (Treanor, 1993). Title V, "Miscellaneous," outlined these key provisions that ultimately provided some of the framework for the future ADA. Those provisions were defined in Sections 501 through 504.

Section 501 supported the creation of an "Interagency Committee on Handicapped Employees," which consisted of members of a variety of federal agencies. Its mission was the assurance that each agency had in place an affirmative action plan for the hiring, placement, and advancement of individuals with disabilities. Section 502 provided support for the creation of the federal Architectural and Transportation Barriers Compliance Board, charged with implementing the physical access provisions of the act by the federal government as well as any program or activity that is financed by the federal government, such as colleges, universities, and health care settings. Section 503 mandates that any federal contractor with a contract that exceeds $2,500 have in place an affirmative action program that seeks to assure the employment and advancement in employment of qualified individuals with disabilities. Section 504 (which consisted of only one sentence) stipulates that

> no otherwise qualified handicapped individual in the United States . . . shall solely by reason of his handicap, be excluded from participation in, be denied the benefits of, or be subjected to discrimination under any program or activities receiving Federal financial assistance or under any program or activity conducted by an Executive agency or by the United States Postal Service. (cited in Treanor, 1993, p. 60)

As initially drafted, the single sentence of Section 504, while exhibiting a shift in stance that rhetorically asserted the civil rights of members of the disability category, needed to be defined, explained, and set in the context of regulatory structure before the philosophical stance was translated into a legitimate response.

The definition of a "handicapped" individual in the Rehabilitation Act was drawn largely from earlier vocational rehabilitation legislation that focused on issues of employment. As such, the term was defined as "any individual who (A) has a physical or mental disability which constitutes a substantial handicap to employment and (B) can reasonably be expected to benefit in terms of employability from vocational rehabilitation services" (cited in Treanor, 1993, p. 86). Within the Department of Heath Education and Welfare (HEW), Office of Civil Rights (OCR), it was determined that the provisions of the Rehabilitation Act extended beyond the areas of employment and included individuals, such as children and older adults, who might not be immediately affected by issues of employability.

To expand response, staff from the OCR and the Senate Subcommittee on the Handicapped met in conference committee. As a result, the earlier definition was broadened under the Rehabilitation Act Amendments of 1974 to mean "any person who (A) has a physical or mental impairment which substantially limits one or more of such person's major life activities, (B) has a record of such impairment, or (C) is regarded as having such impairment" (cited in Treanor, 1993, p. 87).

This change in both stance and scope was significant, as it rendered protection from discrimination and supported the right to access services without regard to the employability of the individual. The clarifications were also important historical markers of the increasing recognition of social and political explanations of atypicality. Additionally, the conference committee made two critical decisions; first, that Section 504 regulations were to be "patterned after the anti-discrimination language of Section 601 of the Civil Rights Act of 1964 and Section 901 of the Educational Amendments of 1972" and, second, that the primary enforcement authority and therefore regulatory development responsibility was "delegated to HEW" (cited in Treanor, 1993, p. 87).

The importance of using the Civil Rights Act of 1964 as a template for antidiscrimination legislation for the disabled category lies in the success of disability activists to join with other protected categorical groups. Moreover, locating regulation in HEW reflected the stance that disability discrimination did not only exist as a denial of access to work but was experienced throughout the life span across many medical diagnostic explanations.

The ADA is the legislative event that legitimates members of disabled categories and affirms that prohibition of discrimination against people with medical explanations of disability is a legitimate response. The purpose of the ADA was written as follows:

> to provide or extend, to the private sector, to persons with disabilities civil rights protections in the areas of employment, public services and transportation, public accommodations, and telecommunications. The ADA is a "clear and comprehensive national mandate to end discrimination against individuals with disabilities and to bring persons with disabilities into the economic and social mainstream of American life" (Harkin, 1990, p. 1).

As revealed by current legal challenges, the legitimacy of medical explanations and scope of the responsibilities of the employment sector continue to becontentious as individuals with increasingly diverse medical diagnostic explanations for atypicality seek legitimacy and protective response under this act.

Because of the importance of technology in advancing both support and civil rights responses to individuals with atypicality explained by some medical diagnoses, we now turn our attention to assistive technology legislation. The

Assistive Technology Act of 1998 (ATA; P.L. 105–394) both extended and broadened its predecessor, the Technology-Related Assistance for Individuals with Disabilities Act of 1988 (Tech Act). The aim of the Tech Act was to increase access to availability of and funding for assistive technology through state efforts and national initiatives. The ATA expanded this aim to include three key provisions: (a) to continue and expand federal financial support to states to sustain and strengthen a permanent comprehensive statewide program of technology-related assistance, (b) to identify the federal policies that facilitate and those that impede the payment for assistive technology devices and services, and (c) to enhance the ability of the federal government to provide states with financial assistance to support information and public awareness programs, improve interagency and public-private coordination, provide technical assistance and training in the provision or use of assistive technology devices and services, and fund national, regional, state, and local initiatives that seek to promote the understanding of and access to assistive technology devices and services.

Additional technology-related legislation was supported by Section 508 of the Rehabilitation Act as amended by Congress in 1998. This section sought to assure that all federal agencies, when they develop procure, maintain, or use electronic and information technology, ensure access to such technology.

As you can see, assistive technology has the capacity to render the atypical as typical. Consider, for example, the use of electronic communication devices. Those with atypical or absent speech can engage in typical communication with the assistance of technology. However, the expense of assistive technology renders it inaccessible to many who might benefit from it. The technology legislation therefore provided not only the service response but also the civil rights of inclusion through financial support necessary for individuals who without technology would not have access to work and community life.

CURRENT CONTEXT

As we see through the legislative history, changes in stance both for defining legitimate criteria for disability categorical membership and for legitimate responses to it occurred throughout the 20th century. Clearly, the effects of civil rights legislation can be seen in the changes in supports and services for individuals with atypicality. For example, in concert with access changes mandated by Section 504 of the Rehabilitation Act, the independent living movement gained momentum during the 1970s and was funded through Title VII of the Rehabilitation Act in 1978 (Braddock, 2001). Founded on the principle that self-determination is a central aspect of personal well-being and based on the view that disability is a result of social attitudes and architectural, legal, and educational barriers that confront people with chronic or permanent medical explanations for atypicality, independent living centers were developed, providing an array of service responses to promote independence that includes peer counseling, driving instruction, home modification consultation, personal assistance referrals, wheelchair repair, job application preparation, and so forth.

The ideology of self-determination continues to be rhetorically reflected in institutional and community responses to disability (Sands & Wehmeyer, 1996). Terms such as "consumer" have replaced labels such as "patient" and "client" to name individuals who obtain disability service responses from some systems. Other legislation, such as the Medicaid Community Attendant Services and Support Act, is pending. If passed, this bill will advance the self-determination and autonomy of individuals by creating a national program of community-based attendant services and supports for all people who are considered legitimately disabled within the definition of the law. Of particular note is the increase in control over services and thus living locations that would be afforded to individuals with legitimate disabilities who currently reside in institutions (ADAPT, n.d.).

The ideologies that guide definitions and responses to disability espouse liberal notions of choice and autonomy along with implicit indications of disabled persons as consumers. However, as we briefly presented in Chapter 1, definitions of disability are not clear, and the tension between disability as an economic phenomenon or the object of charity inheres in policy, legislation, practice, research, and preparation of professionals to work with disabled individuals. Further, as revealed in recent research (DePoy & Werrbach, 1996; National Organization on Disability, 2000; United States Census Bureau, 2002), many individuals with certain medical explanations for atypicality experience disproportionately high poverty, unemployment, high school dropout rates, and exclusion from typical activity and opportunity afforded to those who are not considered disabled.

While there have been significant gains, such as the change in stance asserting that civil rights and economic participation have been denied on the basis of medical diagnosis, the lives of many individuals with atypical activity, appearance, and experience are still compromised with regard to opportunity, autonomy, and self-sufficiency, to name just a few issues. The current scholarship in disability studies reflects both continuing disadvantage and progress in its research and theory. Questions such as the nature of disability, the unity among subpopulations of individuals with diverse medical conditions, competition between those who are legitimately disabled and those who are not in various contexts, and tension created by the intersection of medical hegemony, capitalism, and diversity are all part of the current context of contemporary disability definitions and responses. Moreover, the role of ideology as progressive or regressive is one that requires scrutiny and study. As we proceed through the next chapters, we pose many questions regarding the nature of disability for which we have no absolute answers. Explanatory Legitimacy

Theory and other considerations provide the content and the framework to guide your understanding, analysis, decision making, and action.

SUMMARY

In this chapter, we have identified three major influences on contemporary conceptualizations of the atypical and explanations that qualify for disability designation and treatment: 1. capitalism, 2. growth of science, technology and professional hegemony, and 3. diversity. The intersection of these factors has resulted in the dominance of the medical profession in delimiting the limits of normal, determining what explanations are eligible for disability membership, and shaping the differential responses for category members. We are now prepared to understand the financial context and foundation of disability presented in the next chapter.

FROM BAKE SALE TO COMMODITY

In this chapter, we examine disability from the perspective of economic advantage. Our focus is different from economic explanations of disability that address the way in which atypicality is explained by economic factors, as we look at how diverse interest groups derive economic advantage from disability. An analysis of who benefits from what definitions and approaches to disability can illuminate how the values and efforts of interest groups to position themselves are played out in determining which explanations for atypical activity, appearance, and experience should warrant what type of attention and resources (Davis, 2002; Gill, 1992).

We begin our discussion with a brief application of historical trends to our concern in this chapter. The search for scientific explanations for human experience, including human diversity and difference, along with the statistical concept of "normal" set the stage for medical explanations of disability to emerge and become dominant. Early in the 20th century, when geographic communities were still intact, responding to atypical individuals who were considered worthy of attention was a private concern. Diverse ethnic and cultural groups provided care to individuals who fit the group-specific eligibility (Davis, 2002) criteria for assistance and excluded those who did not. Institutions such as church-related hospitals and nursing homes framed care and assistance as a local obligation rather than a public right. It is important to our discussion to remember that hospitals were initially developed as charitable institutions (Braddock & Parish, 2001; Stiker, 2000).

Given the aims of hospitals and the belief that care for legitimately needy individuals was a moral obligation, charity was the central theme in conceptualizing the care relationship between disabled people and their nondisabled care providers. The provision of assistance to those who met legitimate determinations of worth was therefore supported largely through charitable fundraising or actions (Braddock & Parish, 2001). Individuals with worthy medical explanations for their atypicality were seen as objects of pity, cure, and/or ongoing care. We still see the influence of care as charity in thinking and actions today. We have called this phenomenon the "bake sale" mentality.

The intersection of capitalism, technology, and diversity has been critical particularly in the 20th century to shape how disability is conceptualized and met with resources. Thus, while the notion of disabled individuals as objects of charity and in need of "help" has prevailed and continues its hegemony, it is important to examine this phenomenon within an increasing world of global capitalism. The not-for-profit sector has provided an important structure in which economic benefit can be realized within an ideology of charity.

"Not for Profit": What Does It Mean?

Many of the current agencies that address the needs of disabled individuals are located in the not-for-profit tax classification. The nature of this type of business is both practical and symbolic.

Practically, not-for-profit agencies can access public dollars more easily than for-profit entities (Higgins, 2000). Thus, tax-funded programs such as Medicare and Medicaid, which are seen as public charity for the poor elderly and disabled, provide significant support for the work done through these types of agencies. Charities such as United Way also raise and provide a large part of the financial support for programs serving disabled individuals. Moreover, because there is an implicit reluctance to publicly identify disability services and providers as profiting on the misfortune of those with limitations, service providers often are low paid, even if they possess advanced professional degrees (Friedson, 1980; Starr, 1984). It is not unusual to see fund-raising drives for community agencies that rely on strategies such as the sale of T-shirts, raffles, and, of course, bake sales.

Symbolically, not-for-profit status suggests that disabled individuals are not in the mainstream of the American economy (Gill, 1992; Gleeson, 1997). Let us consider this principle in more detail. Services such as housekeeping, meal preparation, and transportation for many disabled individuals are supported by charity, public dollars, or community efforts. However, for nondisabled counterparts, these services are provided by individuals or companies who are in business to earn a living and profit.

Those providing services to disabled individuals are considered "helpers," while those providing services to nondisabled individuals are employees of profit-making businesses or are self-employed. Clearly, the distinction between helping and working reveals the value of disabled individuals as the object of charity rather than employers or purchasers of service, despite the term "consumer," which has been used to describe disabled individuals who are connected to service systems. This perspective is changing in the early

21st century, as we discuss later in this chapter. For now, consider the Medicaid Community Attendant Services and Supports Act legislation, which provides for individual purchase and control of supports by the disabled individual who qualifies for certain classes of public resources (ADAPT, n.d.). The legislation has been discussed and debated in the U.S. Congress since it was introduced in the early 1990s. However, it has not yet been passed, revealing the opposition on the part of provider lobbies to relinquish control of public dollars and ideologically suggesting that disabled individuals need help and guidance in fiscal decision making.

It is therefore not surprising that the term "helping professions" is used to describe so many of the providers of services to disabled individuals (e.g., rehabilitation personnel, social workers, and so forth). Looking at history of these "helping professions," we see that they emerged from groups of people, primarily women, who were committed to humanistic and charitable treatment of institutionalized individuals. Often portrayed as angels, these women gave of themselves for little or no money to work with disabled individuals. The field of occupational therapy, for example, developed from the work of a small group of people who believed that idle hands created idle minds and took their beliefs into institutions for the "insane" to improve conditions for residents (Levine, 1990; Starr, 1984).

At this point, an excellent question is, Who benefits from conceptualizing disability as the object of moral obligation? There are several analytic approaches that can answer this question.

If we consider the emergence of disability policy, theory, and practice as an issue of ideology, the profound sense of responsibility for individuals whose atypical activity is explained by serendipity or related to giving of oneself at work or war signifies the communal character of caring and collective responsibility (Scotch, 2001; Scotch & Schriner, 1997). Consider the example of Senator Orrin Hatch's (R-UT) support for disability legislation. As a conservative Republican, he supports this legislation despite its alignment with more progressive politics. President George W. Bush's Freedom Initiative is another example of how strange bedfellows such as disability activism mix with a Republican agenda to produce financial opportunity that has a potential benefit for community inclusion.

From a purely fiscal perspective, consider just a few interest groups. First, charities themselves have become big business in the United States. The not-for-profit designation provides a significant tax advantage, while the label implies qualities such as generosity and altruism. Large sums of money are raised by charities where a significant portion often is used for operating expenses, including salaries (Higgins, 2000).

Second, receipt of charity is regulated. Thus, only those who are legitimate under eligibility criteria have the good fortune to be helped. Regulation means that some group has the power to determine resource distribution for another (Bryce, 2000). Therefore, those who are in the regulator's position have much to gain by not-for-profit status.

Third, history informs the symbolic benefit of the charitable approach to disability. As we saw in Chapter 3, the clergy explained the atypical as purposive in that the presence of such individuals provided the venue for laypersons to learn tolerance and altruism. Thus, the roots of contemporary volunteerism and charitable ideology are unearthed and applied to business endeavors, and not-for-profit status signifies altruism. That is, consistent with the Marxist notion that ideology conceals power relationships with acceptable rhetoric (Storey, 1998), companies sporting the not-for-profit label are not readily perceived as opportunistic and exploitive of the unfortunate circumstance of disability despite any profit or financial benefit that is garnered.

DISABILITY AS COMMODITY

Over the past few decades, disability has moved from bake sale to commodity. What do we mean by this? Applying the concepts of commodity and commodification to disability, we note that atypical activity, appearance, and experience take on important roles in Western capitalist culture. A brief, albeit simplified, understanding of commodity can help illuminate this point and the discussion that follows. Although there are many approaches to defining and applying the concept of commodity, a common element is the capitalist exploitation of human experience for the purpose of profit. Consider, for example, the commodity of music. As discussed by philosophers such as Adorno (1941) and Benjamin (1968), music was once an "authentic" activity, that is, one in which individuals directly participated either through creating it or listening to it live. The commodification of this human experience through recording and reproducing music has removed its production from human experience and changed music into a product to be purchased (Benjamin, 1968). In addition to the wide distribution of music to the public for purchase, ownership of the music object can serve as a symbol of economic status, and thus the experience of music making has been supplanted by the symbolic use of music to denote an image (Fussell, 1983).

For some, the process of commodification is pejorative and for others liberating. Consider these two perspectives. Music reproduction makes music available to large masses of individuals who would not have had access to it if it were only in concert halls (Benjamin, 1968). On the other hand, reproduction of human experience removes it from community and human interaction and places it in the arena of economic consumption (Adorno, 1941).

Let us apply these concepts to disability. Think back in history to a time when those with atypical activity, appearance, and/or experience were directly experienced and affected by their communities. The term "disability" did not exist as a categorical symbol, and response to diverse human experience was contained in human interaction. However, disability has become increasingly commodified and is the basis for economic support and profit for many groups.

But what about the notions of reproduction and symbol? How do they apply to disability? As we discussed earlier, disability as a class or category has become an economic symbol for numerous interest groups and for the general public as well.

Let us consider some of the ways in which this has happened. Telethons were among the first media methods to bring the "poster child" symbol into the home and elicit charitable dollars as a result (Gill, 1992; Hahn, 1993). The interaction among typical and atypical was removed from human experience and purchased instead.

Another example of the commodification of disability is the emergence of numerous businesses that provide products specifically for individuals with legitimate disability status. In these areas of production, unlike products for the general public, purchase is regulated by medical or other professional gatekeepers, and the prices of items such as wheelchairs, shower seats, and crutches are inconsistent with the cost of materials, production, and distribution. Payment is assured through insurance dollars for those whose explanations for need are rendered legitimate by providers. For manufacturers, distributors, gatekeepers, and even payers, disability has little to do with its authentic experience but rather signifies economic gain.

Further commodification has occurred in professional training and practice. The sheer number of fields that have developed and that are competing for professional status illustrate the economic gain potential of disability. For example, the initial rehabilitation fields of occupational, speech, and physical therapy have now expanded to include recreation therapy, art therapy, dance therapy, music therapy, and so forth. Each has a professional organization, educational requirements for entry at the graduate level of higher education, restrictive licensure, and assertion of unique scope of practice.

However, as we asserted earlier, we do not believe that commodification is always pejorative or exploitive. The disability rights movement in part has benefited from the expanding awareness of disability issues that result from reproduction. An excellent illustration of this point is the Franklin Delano Roosevelt Memorial in Washington, D.C., in which Roosevelt is portrayed sitting in his wheelchair. The symbol of the atypical as a national leader has been an important signifier of cultural change and increasing acceptance of certain atypical activities, appearances, and experiences among the general public. In addition, disability symbols and spokespeople such as Christopher Reeve, although met with disapproval from some groups espousing disability pride, have gained attention as well as resources.

However, commodification of disability does not occur without negative consequences. Exploitation for profit in the form of inflated prices for adaptive and assistive technology is a common occurrence. We address this point later in this chapter when we examine the changing economics of legitimacy in the 21st century.

Of particular note is the example of sheltered work. While civil rights efforts to eliminate the exploitation of foreign workers have been expanded, the mix of ideology and capitalism has created the forum for the exploitation of individuals with atypical thinking (Gilson, 1998; Sands & Wehmeyer, 1996). Many individuals with mental retardation and other cognitive-diagnostic explanations are frequently employed in sheltered workshops where they do labor such as piecework for large companies at wages far below the minimum. The rationale for prorated pay is founded on in part on views of production and efficiency similar to those advanced by Fredrick Taylor (Kanigel, 1999). Pay in sheltered work is based on measurable output. Because sheltered workshops utilize support staff that are paid, further justification to prorate the wages of the "clients" exists despite the benefit derived by professionals and other "nondisabled" workers who are employed at fair market wages.

The current inclusion ideology asserts that all individuals, including even those with the most severe diagnostic explanations for atypicality, have a right to fully participate in their communities (Coutinho & Repp, 1999). Sheltered workshops are therefore increasingly frowned on by those who espouse inclusion. Supported work has been developed as both an ideology and a practice as a means to provide employment to many individuals who otherwise would not be perceived as employable (Wehman, 2001). This approach places individuals with significant observable atypicalities in mainstream jobs, along with a job coach as needed (Gilson, 1998).

While there are several models of supported employment, all are based on the perceived need for an intermediary between the employer and the disabled individual. Theoretically, the intermediary is incrementally less needed as the disabled individual adjusts to and learns his or her job function. However, this ideal does not usually occur for numerous reasons, not the least of which is the financial benefit received by the professionals and paraprofessionals who provide the "support" (Gilson, 1998). Thus, in concert with theorists such as Althusser (1999), the ideology of inclusion as it is actualized in supported employment maintains capitalism, and disability remains a commodity even in this approach.

Further evidence supporting the commodification of disability is the use of the term "consumer" to replace labels for service users, such as "patient" and "client" (DePoy, 2002). However, as asserted by DePoy, the notion of consumption as choice or even selection of an array of products or services does not fit the public sector euphemism. "Consumer" is most frequently used to describe individuals with atypical thinking explained by diagnoses such as development disability, mental retardation, and autism. Nevertheless, the ascription of the term does indicate that disability is clearly positioned in the fiscal arena. Disability activists and entrepreneurs have capitalized, so to speak, on commodification. We now turn to disability as it enters the economic mainstream.

MOVE TO THE MAINSTREAM

In the past decade, there has been an increasing movement of disability into mainstream business. As we have noted, the groups that have derived primary economic benefit from disability throughout the latter part of the 20th century have been those who provide health and rehabilitation supports and services as well as those with related agendas (e.g., example, insurance, and assistive devices) (Gill, 1992; Gleeson, 1997). However, the intersection of demographic trends and diversity patina has provided a fertile opportunity for disability capitalism to advance into the mainstream. Major new market sectors comprised of disabled individuals have been identified. The aging of the baby boomers has contributed to an increasingly large consumer group with the wealth to make selections among competing products (iCan!, 1999–2002).

Consider the eyeglass industry. While corrective lenses at one time were considered adaptive, the fashion industry has joined with the medical industry to create a multi-million-dollar industry of eyeglasses and related products. Within the disability arena, mobility devices such as canes have entered the mainstream as fashion canes are marketed to individuals through typical venues (iCan!, 1999–2002). Examples of other entrepreneurial efforts marketing to disabled consumers include mainstream magazines such as *WE* (2002), adaptive homes, low-cost loans for adaptive equipment, travel agencies, companies for individuals with mobility impairments, dating agencies for disabled people (ABLEDATA, n.d.), and so forth. Even bank cards, such as VISA, are sporting disability symbols such as Paralympics (VISA, 1996–2001).

Of particular note is the role of technology in the commodification of disability. Think of the number of software manufacturers who are competing for voice-activated programs, screen readers, and products to render computing accessible. Table 4.1 provides a list of on-line Web sites that have moved disability from bake sale to commodity.

While still in its infancy, disability entrepreneurship has the potential to open new markets across the age span. Just the increasing presence of disability studies throughout the academy (Albrecht, Seelman, & Bury, 2001) is evidence that disability has become commodified, is entering the mainstream of capitalist economy and culture, and has been analyzed as such in the emerging theory and research on disability. Similar to Storey's (1998) example of Bob

TABLE

4.1

Accessibility Design Resources
Articles, Books to Buy!, Companies

Accessible Web Page Design Resources
Articles, Books to Buy!, Graphics . . .

Alternative Health/Medicine/Therapies
Alternative Medicine, Alternative Therapies, Books to Buy! . . .

Automotive
Driver rehabilitation programs, Find a vehicle upfitter, Find funding resources . . .

Computer Accessibility Products
Assistive Technology Programs, Augmentative Communication Devices, Books to Buy! . . .

Databases
Find government services in your state

Disabilities Organizations
Advocacy Organizations, Disability-Specific National/International Organizations, Information Organizations . . .

Disabilities/Medical Mailing Lists
Mailing Lists w/WWW Pages, Subscribing to a List, Want to start your own list? . . .

Disabilities/Medical Newsgroups
ALT.*, BIT.LISTSERV.*, MISC.* . . .

Disability File Sources
FTP Sites, Programs by Platform, World Wide Web Sites . . .

Disability Newsletters/Publications

Disability Related Products/Services
Adapted Special Needs Clothing, Assistive Devices/Products for Independent Living, Bed/Comfort Products . . .

Education/University Resources
Books to Buy!, Education Resources, Financial Aid . . .

Free Prescription Medicine

General Disabilities Resources
Books, Books to Buy!, Bulletin Boards/Chat Rooms/IRC . . .

Government/Legislative Disabilities Information
Additional ADA Information, Canadian Disability Resources, Disability Resources by State . . .

Home Automation/Environmental Control
Companies, Information about Home Automation, Microphones . . .

Independent Living
Accessible Housing, Centers, Emergency Assistance . . .

Job Training/Placement/Employment
Books to Buy!,

Legal & Advocacy Resources
Advocacy Resources, Books to Buy!, Legal Resources . . .

Parents
Products, Support

(Continued)

TABLE
4.1 *(Continued)*

Politics

Resources for Caregivers
Books to Buy!, Care Homes/Homecare, Caregiving Resources . . .

Specific Disabilities Resources
Blindness, Cerebral Palsy, Essential Tremor . . .

Spinal Cord Injury Resources
Articles/Pamphlets, Books to Buy!, Bulletin Boards/Chat . . .

Sports Training And Athletic Competition
Books, Equestrian/Horse Riding, and Organizations . . .

Travel and Recreation Resources
Air Travel, Books to Buy!, Destinations . . .

Wheelchair/Mobility Products
Abledata Fact sheets, All-Terrain Wheelchairs, Books to Buy! . . .

Source. iCan! (1999–2002).

Marley (a singer who both dismantled and benefited from capitalism by the reproduction and sale of his music), disability scholars who rail against capitalist control of services, supports, and products for the disabled market also derive benefit from their work within the framework of a capitalist economy.

It is our contention that the application of current thinking such as hegemony theory (Delgado & Stefancic, 1999) to disability is important in that it allows an analysis of disability definitions to be viewed as competing groups and views in negotiation. Thus, the addition of the construct of legitimacy to an understanding of disability and its treatment clarifies how diverse values define and control resources related to the atypical and its explanations.

Consider the examples from U.S. Supreme Court decisions in which employees who filed discrimination claims under the Americans with Disabilities Act (ADA) against employers were debated. Recent decisions upheld the employers' arguments, thus limiting the scope of the ADA in favor of economic considerations (Fawcett & Brantley, 2002).

It is important to remember that the entrance of disability into popular or mass culture has been occurring over the past century. Given the three factors (capitalism, science and technology, and diversity) that we have suggested as primary in how the atypical is explained and treated in current times, it is not surprising that disability is becoming increasingly commodified beyond mere articulation of ideology.

SUMMARY

Disability has moved from the arena of charity into an expanding venue for profit. Initially conceptualized as altruistic help, services for disabled people remain situated in the nonprofit sector. The economic advantage of this location has been realized by numerous industries and provider groups. However, as the atypical becomes more observable and frequent among aging baby boomers, disability is moving into the economic and intellectual mainstream.

two

EXPLANATORY LEGITIMACY THEORY

The historical and economic foundations of disability viewed through the lens of Explanatory Legitimacy Theory have revealed the value-based, purposive, and dynamic nature of human categorization over the centuries. It is therefore not surprising that disability definitions based on medical explanation and judgment have been challenged in academic and scholarly literature despite the continuing dominance of this explanatory framework in education and practice. Consistent with many theorists throughout history, we assert that the multiple definitions of and approaches to disability are important to know, to analyze, and to place in a purposive framework. The importance to us lies in several areas.

First, disability is only one categorical system of human diversity, and thus much of what is discussed in this text is relevant to all categories applied to the range of human experience. Second, understanding categorization as a value judgment and response lays open categorical systems, sometimes presented and understood as static and given, for examination and social change. And while we do not suggest that categories can be eliminated, understanding the value basis for taxonomic decisions and responses makes it possible for the dialogue that is necessary for analysis and social change. Finally, we assert our bias that individuals and groups be seen within the larger context of human diversity and then, when categorization is necessary for community response, capacities, needs, and interests within democratically determined parameters are the delineating factors and that values are clearly articulated. For example, rather than identifying an individual as legitimately disabled and eligible for personal assistant care because of spinal cord injury, the legitimate determination should be made on the basis of what the individual needs to carry out activities of daily living, including transportation to work.

In this section, we detail and illustrate Explanatory Legitimacy Theory as a basis for future testing, analysis, and direction for professional and community change. Before we enter our discussion of theory, we meet four characters who will appear throughout the remainder of book. They use their lives and experiences to ground our analyses and comparisons of diverse approaches to disability definitions, theoretical approaches, and community responses. To expose you to the multiple and different issues faced by members of what is termed "the disability community," the characters represent a broad spectrum of life circumstances. So let us now meet Joshua, Jennifer, Marie, and Robert.

Joshua is now 45 years old. His life has been a series of ups and downs, challenges, and accomplishments. As the first of two children born to Mary and David, much of Joshua's childhood was spent feeling disconnected from his peers and his family, except for his younger sister, Magdalene. Despite their having died at different ages and from different causes, both his parents were active alcoholics. During the later part of his primary school years and then throughout his middle school years, Joshua was engaged in what he terms "minor acts" of juvenile delinquency. Also noteworthy was Joshua's poor performance in school, an important determinant of his future professional direction.

Joshua's use of alcohol increased significantly during high school with regular to daily use/abuse, including periods of increased tolerance, blackouts, driving while drunk (although he was never arrested for such use), increased numbers of hangovers, public intoxication, and a general perception by others that he was an active alcohol abuser. Despite erratic attendance, poor assignment-completion rates, a general attitude of indifference, and periodic assignment to a counseling group, Joshua graduated from high school, but with poor grades and noncompetitive test scores on college entrance examinations. The next four years of his life were marked by several periods of voluntary inpatient and outpatient treatment, along with attendance at several meetings of Alcoholics Anonymous (AA). On his 22nd birthday, Joshua again signed himself into an inpatient county-based alcohol treatment unit. This event marked his first sustained period of abstinence from substance use and his continued participation in AA, and this period of recovery is ongoing today. At the same time, he also attempted to secure vocational rehabilitation services so that he could enroll in college and complete his education. His assigned vocational rehabilitation counselor was very reluctant to support Joshua in seeking an academic degree, documenting in his notes that Joshua was "alcoholic, unreliable, and unprepared due to poor performance in school and on college entrance examinations." Only after insisting that the full treatment team meet, including his vocational counselor, occupational therapist, physician, and social worker, was Joshua able to obtain funding for his plan of recovery and sustained and substantive employment. Over the course of his efforts at recovery, his work to pursue the goals he wanted, and his undergraduate course work, Joshua developed an interest in political science and public policy, leading him to major in political science and a minor in public policy. During his senior year, reflecting back on the critical role that school performance had on his life, Joshua decided to pursue a joint degree in social work and law with a practice focus on public policy and particular attention to public education law and policy. Joshua worked in a variety of capacities, including two years spent as the attorney for the Disability Rights Center in a small city in the southeastern United States. Ultimately, he ran for office and championed educational reform for all students. At 35 years of age, Joshua began to notice increasing fatigue and difficulty with vision but passed it off as stress and aging. He went to the pharmacy and bought a pair of reading glasses, which magnified print enough for him to see, even though it still was blurry. About one year following the onset of fatigue, Joshua was driving at night and was stopped by the police. Another driver, seeing Joshua's erratic driving, called the police and suggested that the operator of the car might be drunk. The officer, observing Joshua try to walk a straight line, noticed Joshua's poor coordination, checked his record, and asked Joshua to go to the police station to take a Breathalyzer test. When Joshua's wife arrived at the police station to drive Joshua home, she learned that Joshua had not been drinking alcohol and admitted that she was fearful over the past few months that he had resumed drinking but was afraid to confront him. That evening was a turning point for Joshua. He realized that his history of alcoholism would always be present, albeit distant and not a concern for him. Joshua immediately made an appointment with his general practitioner, who sent Joshua to a neurologist. After seeing many specialists and undergoing many diagnostic tests, a diagnosis of multiple sclerosis was made.

As a result of complications from polio, Jennifer's primary education was divided between classes at the hospital and home schooling, with her father and mother acting as her teachers using textbooks provided by the local public school district. When not in the hospital, Jennifer was often confined to her home because of either the immobility created by her various leg and body casts or the lack of accessibility to classes at her elementary school. At the elementary school, the fourth-, fifth-, and sixth-grade classes were held on the second floor of a building that did not have an elevator. Fortunately for Jennifer, her middle school was on only one level, with just a few steps up to the front entrance. The back of the building, however, was ramped to allow workers, delivery people, and cafeteria staff to bring equipment, supplies, and foodstuff into the building. Although the building housing Jennifer's high school had two stories, she could select classes that were held in classrooms on the first floor. One of the big problems for Jennifer during high school was trying to convince school administrators, her teachers, and the guidance counselor that she wanted to attend college and therefore would need college prep courses. Unfortunately, many of these classes were offered only in classrooms on the second floor. Jennifer's mother and father had been very active in the parent-teacher association. Because of the level of their activity, Jennifer's parents had learned how to "work" with school officials, including the school board, to push the school district to meet Jennifer's educational needs. Much of her public school education took place prior to the formulation of regulations in 1978 resulting from the Rehabilitation Act of 1973, and her bachelor's and master's degrees were awarded prior to the enactment of the Americans with Disabilities Act of 1990; therefore, Jennifer's educational experiences have included little in the way of accommodation to her disability despite her significant mobility impairments. Following receipt of her doctoral degree in 1995, she secured a position as a teacher in a public high school in her community. At age 44, Jennifer has begun to experience a variety of new musculoskeletal symptoms.

Marie, the third of three daughters for Mr. and Mrs. Hernandez, was born with Down syndrome. Marie's introduction to the health care system actually began prior to her birth. Following amniocenteses and a sonogram, at five months' gestation, the Hernandezes were informed by their physician not only of the sex of the fetus but also of the likelihood that the child, if born, would be born with a lifelong cognitive condition. In addition to discussing the "situation" with their physician, the Hernandezes were referred to the social worker, Bill, at the local hospital-based developmental clinic. In what amounted to several meetings with the social worker, the Hernandezes explored a full range of possible social, political, economic, emotional, and personal implications of giving birth to and raising a child with an identified medical condition resulting in mental retardation. Although a variety of options and possibilities were presented, the Hernandezes steadfastly and without question rejected abortion as potential "medical intervention." In addition to the information and insight that the social worker provided, once the Hernandezes told family members and very close friends that Mrs. Hernandez was pregnant, advice, comments, suggestions, and expressions of both joy and "sorrow" seemed to come from both expected and unexpected sources. That some friends and even some family members would express sorrow at the prospect of Mrs. Hernandez's giving birth to a child with mental retardation seemed not only odd but hurtful as well.

Following the birth of Marie, one of the first health care providers to stop by the Hernandezes and Marie was the social worker from the developmental clinic. This time, Bill came with information about the local infant early intervention program. With their introduction to this program and early intervention services and resources, the Hernandezes were introduced to the world of intervention and treatment planning outlined in the individual family service plan (IFSP). Professionals, including occupational therapists, physical therapists, recreation therapists, psychologists, and speech therapists, evaluated and provided intervention for Marie, with the focus on increasing her readiness for school. As the years progressed and Marie grew old enough to enter primary school, these intervention and treatment plans shifted from being called IFSPs to individual education plans (IEPs). Although many of the individuals who had been involved with Marie and her family before she entered school no longer were involved in making assessments, conducting evaluations, and suggesting and providing interventions or "treatments," they were replaced by other individuals whose roles and activities were similar. Although for the Hernandezes raising Marie was much like raising their other two daughters, Melissa and Wanda, there was much about their involvement with and connection to Marie that was quite different. At each parent-teacher conference for Melissa and Wanda, only three people were at the meeting: Mr. and Mrs. Hernandez and the teacher. At these conferences, they discussed a variety of topics, but much of the time was spent reviewing the progress of Melissa and Wanda as students, planning for assignments that would follow, and discussing for whose class Melissa or Wanda should sign up the following year. When Melissa and Wanda entered middle school, the planning focused on which classes to take, possible career paths, and what high school might be like for each of them.

Parent-teacher conferences for Marie were much more involved and much more complicated. Rather than taking place during the later part of each semester, the meetings for Marie took place at the beginning and the end of the year. These meetings, rather than involving only the Hernandezes and Marie's teacher(s), included a variety of providers, with a significant part of the conference (IEP meeting) focusing on Marie's cognitive impairment and the perceived impact of the associated and presumed limitations of her current diagnostic status on her capability to actively participate in her education.

Robert grew up in a poor urban environment, and at the age of 18, he enlisted in the Air Force in 1939. He was trained as a navigator and thus spent many hours in the air, plotting and maintaining courses for aerial defense. On January 25, 1944, while flying over Panama, an electrical malfunction occurred, causing a flash fire under Robert's seat. Although the plane landed safely, Robert was injured. He sustained second- and third-degree burns on his arms, face, and trunk and lost the sight in his left eye. Against his will, he returned home for rehabilitation. The Air Force physician proclaimed Robert disabled, and Robert was honorably discharged from the Air Force in 1944. After the war, Robert used his veterans' benefits to support himself in school. He graduated from the local technical college with a certification in air conditioner and refrigerator repair. He supported his family by working full time at his own repair business and retired in 1986 at the age of 65. Although he had wanted to continue working, he noticed that he was having difficulty hearing the machines and thus felt that he was no longer able to maintain the quality of his work.

Now let us follow Joshua, Jennifer, Marie, and Robert into the theoretical world of Exploratory Legitimacy Theory and then back into their lives in the community in Section 3.

The Descriptive Element of Explanatory Legitimacy Theory

In this chapter, we explore the descriptive element of Explanatory Legitimacy Theory. As we introduced in Chapter 1, description is comprised of activity, appearance, and experience. Activity refers to what people do, how they do it, and what they do not do throughout their lives. We now further clarify activity as observable. Observable description also includes appearance (how people look to others). Experience (one's personal and unique ways of being, articulating, and sensing) is the reportable element of description. Later in this chapter, we provide more detail and illustration. For now, let us think of observables as activity and appearance that can be ascertained directly and agreed on by more than one observer. Reportables are experiences that are not directly ascertainable and must be inferred or asserted by the "experiencer."

By analytically examining and then building on relevant literature, we advance our organizational framework of description. We suggest that human activity, appearance, and experience span a full range of diversity and have been categorized as typical and atypical. How the distinction is made between the two depends on many factors, some of which we present through our analysis of the primary literature informing disability.

Theoretical Foundations of Description

The questions of what people do, how they appear, and what they experience have been approached and answered in many ways by philosophers, social scientists, theologians, and others. Although we cannot cover all the theories on human description, in this chapter we examine those that have been most relevant to our discussion of the typical and the atypical.

We begin with human development literature, which has provided a prolific, influential body of knowledge regarding normal and not-normal human existence. Perhaps the most famous of the developmental theorists was Sigmund Freud. Focusing on psychosexual development, he and those who built on his theories posited that all individuals were intrinsically predetermined to unfold in typical ways through a series of normative stages. Deviations from those stages were a function of pathological family relations, or, for post-Freudian theorists, dysfunction in the interaction between the developing individual and his or her emotional-social context (Davis, 2002; Hutchison, 1999).

A very simple psychoanalytic examination of Joshua might identify his adolescent atypical activity of excessive alcohol intake as orally motivated, resulting from his ineffective navigation of the oral stage of development in his infancy. Through looking at his relationship with parents or caregivers, his abnormal excess would be explained and an appropriate plan devised to help Joshua understand and remediate his oral excess.

Theorists such as Piaget who addressed human thinking adopted similar deterministic approaches to diverse domains of human activity. We will not detail the theoretical frameworks in this book since there are so many excellent texts that elucidate human development theory. However, we bring developmental theories to your attention to make some important points about stances on what people do, how they do it, and what they do not do.

Initial developmental stage theories were developed by conducting research on humans and using observations of human activity at specific ages across the life span to determine what was characteristic, frequent, and therefore normal (Davis, 2001). From these theories, based on observation or theoretical inference of "what is," norms were developed and applied to "what should be." In essence, what is now asserted as desirable in human performance, appearance, and experience is based on what the majority of people did during systematic observation. Deviance was therefore defined as outside the limits of normal (Davis, 2001; Hutchison, 1999). Consider each of our characters. Each falls outside of, and is described relative to, what is typical. Joshua's youth was characterized by excessive alcohol use. The word "excessive" implicitly refers to a norm. Similarly, rather than being described as a wheelchair user, Jennifer is referred to by her teachers and peers as an individual with a mobility impairment, Marie is considered below the standard for normal intelligence, and Robert can be described by vision and hearing loss. Each character is therefore described in comparison to what is frequent, typical, and expected.

Interestingly, Freud developed his theories of normal psychosexual development largely on the basis of data from his clinical practice (Freud, 1978), and Piaget theorized cognitive development on the basis of inferences about the observations of his own children (Mussen, 1983).

Because many theories are retrospective, being based on inference about the meaning of observed performance and applied to groups who did not take part in the research and theory development, many theorists challenged

The normal curve

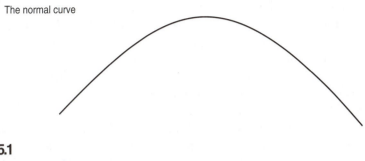

Figure 5.1

The Normal Curve

traditional stage theories. Behaviorists posited that theories inferred from abstract indicators of human activity were based on untrustworthy evidence. In response, they developed theories in which a direct or a mediated reaction to environmental stimuli was observed and recorded. These studies gave rise to notions of human behavior as a response in total or in part to external factors and influences (Hutchison, 1999). For example, Joshua's career choice might be considered a response to his own school environment, and Robert's retirement might be considered a response framed by social expectations that one retire rather than change the nature of work to meet one's changing body.

These two primary approaches to characterizing human description have formed the foundation for current views of what is typical and atypical even with the increasing attention to diversity patina and depth correlates, including but not limited to race, ethnicity, geography, class, and socioeconomic status. Moreover, basic developmental theories form the foundation for standardized testing in multiple domains of human activity, appearance, and experience (Aylward, 1994).

Consider Marie. In third grade, all students in her school district were tested for intelligence, reading, and math with standardized assessments. Items for the test were based on current theories of child development. Based on the normal curve illustrated in Figure 5.1, those scoring at the extremes of the curve were considered atypical and treated as such in school. Those scoring below the norm, including Marie, were placed in special education classes, and those scoring above were placed in classes for gifted students. As you can see by this example, theory defines what is typical and underpins not only testing but also the actions taken on the basis of that testing.

Anthropology has advanced another important way of looking at humans. Classical anthropological research relied on ethnographic inquiry to infer and then characterize typical practices and the explicit and tacit rules that governed them. Classical anthropologists immersed themselves in unknown groups that they named "cultures" to observe activity as the basis for discovering the boundaries and characteristics of that particular culture, including criteria for membership, kinship, roles, language, symbols, rituals, traditions, and rules of behavior (Lévi-Strauss, 2000).

Ethnographic research methods and variations thereof have been applied more recently to characterize norms and expectations within familiar cultures, such as the teen culture and rural cultures in the United States.

Although culture has multiple definitions, here we define it as a construct that attributes shared identity, language, tacit rules, symbols, rituals, and expectations to all members of a specific group. Ethnographic inquiry among other narrative and theory-building approaches has been instrumental in defining cultural norms and distinguishing culturally specific differences in what is considered typical among diverse groups. Feminist researchers have relied largely on theory-building strategies of inquiry to characterize gendered differences in all areas of human activity, appearance, and experience (Hanson, 2002).

Culturally sensitive approaches to examining human description specify cultural norms and membership rules and distinguish these from atypicalities and nonmembership (Ingstad & Whyte, 1995). Theory emerging from this type of inquiry has been influential in making the atypical typical, meaning that phenomena considered atypical through the lens of traditional human development theories and founded on evidence derived from mainstream cultures can be examined and characterized as typical for those who do not fit the characteristics of the mainstream research samples (DePoy & Gitlin, 1998).

To illustrate, we use an example from Robert's initial hearing evaluation. The audiologist received a referral to assess Robert's hearing. In observing Robert's interaction with other people in the audiology clinic, the audiologist noted that Robert was animated to the point of agitation in his gestures and was violating the physical space of other patients. The audiologist wondered whether Robert's atypical behavior might be due to dementia that would result in poor social judgment. She wrote this note in Robert's chart for further follow-up. However, in speaking with Robert's family members later in the week when they all came to receive the results of the hearing test, the audiologist noticed that all of them were behaving in the same manner. She learned that this type of gesturing was characteristic of the ethnic culture of this family. She amended her notes—with humility and having learned much.

In addition to ethnicity, variables that have been considered to influence norms and deviations thereof include but are not limited to geographic location, race, class, gender, socioeconomic status, and the role of the environment in affecting individual activity (Harrison & Huntington, 2001). Theory and knowledge that capture and characterize typical and atypical have reflected the recognition of the importance of these diversity patina and depth variables.

However, we also caution you that the assumption of differences related to what we have termed "diversity patina" without verification is as problematic as the application of theory in circumstances in which it is irrelevant or inaccurate. Gould (1996) illustrates in his book *The Mismeasure of Man* how diversity patina in the form-specific observable characteristics of immigrants who came through Ellis Island (such as a protruding brow and dark eyebrows) was used as inferential evidence to signify limited intelligence. Thus, the mere presence of these characteristics was attributed to a meaning of "cognitive deficiency" and resulted in placement in state schools despite one's capacities.

Consider the exclusion of women from men's competitive sports. While it may be accurate to say that most women could not compete with men in professional football, using gender rather than skill as a means to make that decision illuminates how diversity patina can be used to exclude and even unintentionally discriminate.

Until now, we have been examining human description from the perspective of the whole person. Much of the literature that informs notions of human phenomena is also derived from examining the appearance and function of specific body parts and systems. For example, human biology is usually approached by learning about organs and systems—such as the neurological, cardiovascular, musculoskeletal, reproductive, and sensory—and their component structures and functions (Gilson, in Hutchison, 1999). This knowledge forms the basis for notions of typical growth, aging, and biological functioning. Determination of the atypical is made if appearance or function deviates from what is most frequently observed.

Consider Jennifer here. Her initial assessment as mobility impaired and her subsequent treatment as a child was based on her musculoskeletal and neurological atypicalities. Thus, access to the environment was not addressed since provider scope was limited to treatment of atypical biological structures and functions.

We therefore can look to disciplines such as biology, microbiology, psychology, anatomy, and so forth for delimited descriptions of component parts of human description. Deviations from those typical structures, depending on how extreme, have been characterized from birth defects to freakish body characteristics (Garland-Thomson, 1996). For this reason, Robert underwent significant plastic surgery to reduce the scarring from burns and to improve the cosmetic appearance of his face. As Davis (2002) suggests, the notion of normal body has resulted in the cultural acceptance of practices and industries, including health care, nutrition, exercise, cosmetics, and so forth, all designed to fashion bodies within the norm. Hanson (2002) goes farther to suggest that biological categorization is inaccurate, reductionist, and potentially discriminatory.

On the other end of the spectrum from biological elements, systems theory describes humans in context. Typical interaction between individuals and systems is a central tenet that can be characterized and codified, and any deviations therefore can be classified as atypical (von Bertalanffy, 1969). The size and scope of systems can vary greatly from universal systems to family systems. Much of the knowledge that underpins family therapy practice relies on definitions of functional and dysfunctional family systems (Carter, McGoldrick, & Ferraro, 1989).

Consider Joshua and Marie as examples. We learned that one major area of atypical activity that affected Joshua's atypical alcohol consumption was his family interaction. Contrasted to what is considered desirable in family systems relations, Joshua and his family were certainly outside those boundaries. If we look at Marie in her school system, the typical manner in which she interacts with the teacher, other students, and expected achievements render her atypical in the public learning system.

The humanities and other science disciplines, such as engineering, describe and reflect human activity, appearance, and experience in ways that differ from the biological and social sciences and professions that rely on that knowledge base. For example, performing arts provide a forum for the visible depiction of humans. In the visual arts, we can infer much about the artist and the context in which the artist created the work. Leonardo da Vinci was a humanist who created a visual of the human form that represented what most of us consider accurate. However, we attended an exhibit in which human portraits were painted as genetic structures. Both works of art (da Vinci's and the one at the exhibit) were devoted to characterizing the human form, each influenced by the context in which the work was created.

Appearance itself has also been studied and discussed extensively in diverse bodies of literature. The judgment regarding typical and atypical appearance of bodies, body parts, and mannerisms and adornments is context bound (Davis, 2002; Garland-Thomson, 1996; Mitchell & Snyder, 2001). Criteria for beauty, looking healthy, dressing appropriately, and so forth are specific to cultures, subgroups, and contexts and are normative (Davis, 2002). For example, consider the contextual changes in conceptions about healthy bodies, obesity, cleanliness, and even the health of specific body parts or systems, such as women's musculature (Mitchell & Snyder, 2001). An article in the *New York Times* is an excellent example of how criteria regarding beauty change. The article discussed the opposition of one woman to the widespread use of a skin-lightening product by women in South Africa (Lacey, 2002). As we have discussed for observable activity, what is typical and atypical in appearance depends on one's stance.

Professional knowledge which informs assessment and treatment is based on notions of typical and atypical from the collective and relevant theoretical literature. For example, occupational therapists who claim human activity as their domain of concern have founded practice on literature from human development, biology, and, more recently, anthropology and other narrative inquiry (Kielhofner, 2002). From an occupational therapy stance, Marie would be assessed for her function in daily occupations (purposive activities), roles, and interests (Early, Neistadt, & Crepeau, 1999; Kielhofner, 2002). Intervention would be focused on using purposive activity to promote normal functioning.

Medicine and nursing rely heavily on human biology, physiology, anatomy, and psychology as well as chemistry and its subspecialties. Each uses theoretical lenses through which to view human activity, appearance, and experience and to distinguish between typical and atypical. As a child, Marie may have been assessed by the physician by blood, urine, and physical tests as a basis for confirming the diagnosis of Down syndrome. Any medications for related symptoms (such as seizures) would be prescribed in response to medical findings. Nursing intervention might be directed to Marie's parents, helping them maintain the health of their child.

Of particular relevance to our discussion of the descriptive element of Explanatory Legitimacy Theory is the International Classification of Functioning (ICF). The ICF is the most recent revision of the International Classification of Functioning and Disability (ICIDH-2) (Ustun et al., 2002), a classification system that uses activity to distinguish among health, illness, impairment, and disability. Until the most recent versions, the ICIDH was criticized for its negligence of contextual influences on health and/or disability. Recognizing the ill fit of this categorical assessment with increasingly diverse populations, the need for a multidimensional, universal approach to assessment was asserted and undertaken (Ustun et al., 2002).

To accomplish this complex task, cross-cultural applicability research (CAR) was chosen as a method to conduct inquiry supporting the revision of the ICIDH. CAR is a multimethod approach to inquiry that is based on the following heuristics:

> The context of the experience is a critical variable.
> Individuals experience phenomena in diverse ways.
> Prediction of human experience is multidimensional (individual, interactive, social, and cultural).
> Transferring an existing assessment protocol from one culture or subgroup to another is not reasonable without systematic study.
> Screening must include assessment of positive (occurring) and negative (absent) phenomena.
> Universal assessment takes into account that the phenomenon being assessed is experienced differently among diverse groups.
> Psychometric rigor is critical for accuracy of assessment and screening.
> Instrumentation should always leave room for continuous updating.

TABLE 5.1   ACTIVITIES

1 Learning and applying knowledge
2 General tasks and demands
3 Communication
4 Mobility
5 Self-care
6 Domestic life
7 Interpersonal interactions and relationships
8 Major life areas
9 Community, social, and civic life

The ICF approaches measurement with four descriptive categories:

Activity—Defined as the execution of a task or action by an individual
Activity limitations—Defined as difficulties in executing activities
Participation—Conceptualized as involvement in a life situation
Participation restrictions—Problems an individual may experience in involvement in life situations (Ustun et al., 2002)

Thus, similar to Explanatory Legitimacy Theory and informing our theoretical approach to description, the ICF relies on observed or reported typical and atypical activity as the basis for judgments about human well-being. Listed next are the activity categories that the ICF's developers have agreed on as universal. (See Table 5.1.)

Each of these broad categories is broken into subcategories and tasks, and the descriptive element of health is determined by the nature of one's capacity to act in a manner typical for his or her reference group in a hypothesized standard environment, one that would not influence the activity in any way. Capacity is then compared to expected performance and assessed along with contextual correlates to determine the efficacy of an individual's activity. Using the ICF, Joshua might be seen as limited in mobility and major life areas (vision) at the onset of multiple sclerosis. However, his strengths, including his ability to continue his work, domestic life, and other interactions, would be noted as well as the limitations. He might be assessed in multiple environments, such as those with hot and cold temperatures, to look at the effect of temperature control on his symptoms.

The value of the ICF in assessing disability has been debated and remains a point of contention among providers and researchers (Pfeiffer, 1998). However, the methodological approach, the descriptive element, and the intent to factor contextual variables into measurement represent advancements on which to build.

A limitation that we have noted is the combination of observables and reportables. Let's consider Marie. Using the ICF and on the basis of her diagnosis and various standardized testing protocols, we might see her as limited in her ability to learn and apply knowledge. However, the extent to which her communication skills on tests, test-taking capacity, and other variables are responsible for her limited performance in learning and applying knowledge is not known and must be inferred on the basis of theory.

Building on the literature and taking into account what we believe to be important and missing from current taxonomies of human phenomena, we have divided description into two categories: observables and reportables. We discuss these now in more detail.

OBSERVABLES

Observables are defined as activity and appearance that are visible or ascertainable by direct assessment and agreement among observers. We have synthesized the activity categories from the ICF with activity classifications from the occupational performance framework posited by Kielhofner (2002) to derive the following observable activity categories:

Self-care—Hygiene, toileting, feeding, and maintaining health and safety

Work—Preparing for and/or engaging in earning, economic, and in-kind contribution or production (including unpaid home care and child care)

Play—Recreation activity

Rest—Sleep, relaxation for the purpose of health maintenance

Transportation—Mobility activity with or without assistance, including moving in one's immediate environment or from one environment to another by car, bus, and so forth

Social relating—Interacting with others at all levels, including intimacy, family, and community

Worship—Attending or participating in spiritual activity

Citizenship—Civic activity distinguished from work, including volunteering, voting, and so forth

In Box 5.1 on the next page, the revisions were made in an effort to clarify activities and distinguish the categories more sharply from one another. In Explanatory Legitimacy Theory, we do not provide absolute definitions of typical and atypical activity in each category but rather suggest that description is comprised of a continuum of diversity. Further, we do not claim that all categories are or should be present in the lives of all individuals. The categories are designed primarily to structure observation of the complexity of human description.

5.1 *Categories of Observable Activity*

Let's turn to Jennifer for an example. Considering transportation, we might describe Jennifer's activity as follows: Jennifer uses a wheelchair for mobility and thus must use accessible public transportation in order to travel distances. She requires accessible (for wheeled mobility) entrance and egress to navigate buildings and accessible pathways to navigate space.

REPORTABLES

Reportables are defined as human experience. That which is directly reported or inferred fits under this descriptive subcategory. Building on the ICF and theoretical tenets from multiple sources of literature, we have organized reportable experience into the following categories listed in Box 5.2

The only way we can ascertain Marie's thinking and knowledge is to infer them from what she communicates or does. If she chooses not to or is unable to communicate her thinking and knowledge, only she experiences it. Similarly, only Robert can experience his own pain, while we can only infer it from his actions or reports or our assumptions.

We make the distinction between observables and reportables because of its critical contribution to the analysis of descriptions of human phenomena. The existence and nature of reportables have been much more contentious than that which is observable, given that indirect evidence is the basis for any theory or belief about reportables. Whereas observables can be verified through the agreement of those who are observing, inferences and thus reportables cannot. We can only postulate about the existence of constructs such as intelligence, insanity, perception, spirituality, and so forth.

Philosophers have been concerned with these reportables over the centuries. Extreme opinions, such as those held by Sophists, suggested that one can know only his or her own reality, while positivists suggested a monistic view of reality that could be known by only one type of investigation, namely, the scientific method (Durant, 1991).

Different from observables, reportables leave open significant room for doubt, thus the tension between those with visible and nonvisible atypicalities in asserting and/or denying disability legitimacy. Consider Joshua here. Those who knew him in his youth might infer that his atypical mobility is an indication of intoxication, while the explanation for his recent ataxia is the weakness caused by the medical diagnosis of multiple sclerosis. The value on inferred

5.2

Sensing—Hearing, seeing, feeling (e.g., pain, well-being, moving through space, and touch), tasting, and smelling

Perceiving—Internally organizing sensory input

Emoting—Loving, hating, and so forth

Believing—Thinking that something is true

Thinking—Cognition

Knowing—Possessing information

Understanding—Agreeing with one or more individuals on the interpretation or meaning of a phenomenon

explanations for his ataxia by his family and colleagues is extremely important for his job and sense of well-being. Thus, while mobility is observable, weakness is reportable, as is intoxication, at least until measured. Even then, the measures may be based on inference in that weakness is often inferred from performance on a task. Thus, because of the reportable nature of possible causes along with Joshua's history, there is much room for explanatory doubt, inaccurate assumption, and potential harm to Joshua.

As you can see by our descriptive categories, we make no judgment about what is typical or atypical, and we do not use the term "function" to describe our stance on human activity. We have tried to be exhaustive and as mutually exclusive for clarity and ease of use in theory, research, professional practice, and promotion of social justice responses for the diversity of human activity, appearance, and experience.

SUMMARY

In this chapter, we have provided an overview of the scholarly pluralism in investigating and characterizing human activity, appearance, and experience. On the basis of the literature and building on current taxonomic organizations of human description, we divided human description into observables and reportables and provided a taxonomy of each. The distinction between reportables and observables was then highlighted as an important element in classical and current theory and in the characterization of human phenomena. We concluded with a discussion of the importance of thinking about observables and reportables with regard to legitimacy value and response.

EXPLANATIONS

We have made the distinction between description and explanation and suggested that the definitional clarity of disability could be improved if these two elements were treated as related but distinct. In this chapter, we focus our attention on explanations for description that have been important in defining disability and responses to it both historically and contemporarily. As the second element of Explanatory Legitimacy Theory, the explanatory dimension provides the rationale for human description. It is this dimension on which value judgments regarding legitimacy are made.

Multiple and often competing explanations for what people do, how they look, and what they experience have been posited in contemporary disability studies literature. We introduced these explanations as two grand categories: medical-diagnostic and constructed. Although we reduced multiple explanations in Chapter 1, in this chapter we recast an expansive net. Moving beyond a cursory distinction between medical and social explanations of disability is critically important to understanding the perspectives both in themselves and as the basis for value judgment. As you read, you might note that many of the explanations seem similar to and overlapping of several others. However, we will point out the important differences and examine how even shades of difference in explanations for atypicality influence legitimacy. We now turn to the medical-diagnostic grand category to compare and contrast the rationales that make up this category.

MEDICAL-DIAGNOSTIC EXPLANATION

The medical-diagnostic explanation for atypical activity, appearance, and experience locates the cause within the individual's physiology as a permanent impediment with diminished capability (Gilson & DePoy, 2002). As a form of biological determinism, the focus in this explanation is on physical, behavioral, psychological, cognitive, and/or sensory tragedy, and thus the problem to be addressed by intervention services is situated within the individual as well (Mackelprang & Salsgiver, 1999; Shakespeare & Watson, 1997).

Consider Joshua's youth. If we accept the explanation for Joshua's atypical alcohol consumption as a medical diagnosis of alcohol dependence, then the solution for it lies in total abstinence. Because the diagnoses of alcohol dependence and addiction are considered physiological dependencies resulting in the compulsion to consume alcohol to the point of inebriation or even unconsciousness, the only interceptive response must be the removal and prohibition of the alcoholic substance from the body. This abstinence, while supported by social and possibly chemical assistance, is the sole responsibility of the individual with the diagnosis.

If we look at Joshua's current atypicalities, low vision, and clumsy walking, the medical condition of multiple sclerosis is explanatory, and intervention would focus on symptom reduction through medication and possibly even suggesting that Joshua move to a cool climate to improve his medical status.

Within the grand medical-diagnostic category, there are numerous subcategories. In this chapter, we discuss two: medical explanations and rehabilitation explanations.

Medical Explanation

Medical explanations for atypicality posit that recognizable pathology causes the atypical (Mackelprang & Salsgiver, 1999; Shakespeare & Watson, 1997). In order to explain an atypical phenomenon, the medical provider or team observes an individual; determines whether the activity, appearance, and/or experience exceeds what is considered to be "within normal limits"; amasses necessary observable or inferred evidence through accepted assessment procedures; and makes a determination regarding the degree to which the evidence fits a particular diagnostic category. Although there are many variations on this approach, such as public health explanations that focus on groups and communities rather than individuals, the medical stance explains atypicality from the perspective of health and illness (Gilson & DePoy, 2000).

Interventions that proceed from medical explanations are designed ideally to be curative. That is, services are aimed at lessening or correcting the condition, provided that the patient or patient group complies with professional direction. Pharmaceuticals, health behavior, and other methods designed to limit pathology and enhance health may also be part of the interventive approach (Gilson & DePoy, 2000).

If Jennifer were to consult a physician, the most likely object of discussion, observation, diagnosis, and treatment would be musculoskeletal changes related to postpolio syndrome.

For the most part, the medical explanation is determined by a medical professional on the basis of specialized knowledge that is held by that professional group. As indicated by Quinn (1998), an important element of the medical explanation relevant to disability determination is Parson's (1956) notion of illness in which the illness begets a set of behavioral expectations many of which excuse the sick person from expected and desired role behaviors. In exchange for relinquishing obligations, the individual who is ill, or in our case disabled, is expected to be compliant with and appreciative of medical intervention(s) designed to cure or help. The implicit view of the disabled human in the medical explanation is therefore consistent with the historical perspective of the individual as object of charity or help. Moreover, any individual or group whose diagnosis fits the legitimate criteria for disability is expected to be both willing to listen to authority and thankful for the intervention offered by knowledgeable professionals in exchange for assistance.

Let us consider Marie for illumination of this important point. When Mrs. Hernandez had the amniocentesis, an automatic response on the part of social service was triggered. The knowledgeable social worker provided information to Mr. and Mrs. Hernandez. The decision to proceed with pregnancy and birth provided the rationale for professional intervention in all arenas of Marie's life, including her education. Formal plans in which medical and social service professionals had a major influence were mandated for Marie on the basis of her medical diagnosis of Down syndrome. In exchange for the publicly funded help, the expectation is that the family will be ready-and-willing participants in the process, compliant with the outcome of the formal planning process, and thankful.

For Jennifer, diagnostic explanation would be followed by Jennifer's compliance with a medical treatment regimen of medication and healthy behavior, and for Robert, medical intervention would most likely be aimed at improving his hearing and remaining vision.

While there has been some change, both rhetorically and in practice, the notions of charity and compliance are endemic to medical explanations of atypicality (Charlton, 1998; Shapiro, 1990). They hold professionals as knowers and provide the physiological rationale for mandated intervention, such as the early intervention that was immediately present in Marie's life.

Not unexpectedly, the medical explanation is not popular among many people with diagnoses that are considered permanent or that cannot be cured, modified, or changed even by professional intervention (Quinn, 1998). In this view, the individual with the medical explanation who is not "responsive" to a defined intervention remains pathological or deficient.

Consider Jennifer's life prior to legislation mandating access to public education. Her atypical mobility, explained by a medical-diagnostic cause, was not curable, and thus she had to accept her exclusion from public education. As a result of a permanent internal medical explanation, Jennifer was seen as deficient and could not actualize the same educational rights of those who exhibited the standard, acceptable criterion of mobility activity necessary to participate in public education.

Similarly, Robert's scarring, although reduced by surgery, is a residual and permanent atypicality in appearance that carries an undesirable diagnosis that cannot be cured.

Rehabilitation Explanation

The rehabilitation explanation falls under the rubric of medical-diagnostic explanation but is more focused in scope. From this stance, the individual's atypical activities are explained not only by their diagnosis but also by the degree to which that diagnostic condition is thought to pose barriers to performance or behavior in what are considered contextually embedded normative life roles (Gilson & DePoy, 2000).

The term "function" is used profusely throughout the rehabilitation explanation to denote acceptable and efficacious human performance in expected, appropriate, and typical life roles, ages, phases, and/or stages, depending on the theoretical frame of reference used to establish the criterion for function. Remember that we expressed our reluctance to use the term "function" as descriptive. Now you can see why. When we analyze the meaning of function, we see that while it contains a descriptive element (that of doing), accepted and unaccepted methods of doing within delimited contexts inhere within the concept.

Consider Marie again. As we saw in her history, Marie was able to "function" in the regular classroom until third grade. By that we mean that she was able to perform the activities expected of her age level within acceptable or normal limits. However, when her age cohorts surpassed Marie in reading skill, Marie was no longer sufficiently functional in order to be maintained in her class during reading time. Falling below the cutoff criterion for inclusion in regular reading education, Marie was placed in special education and remedial reading classes.

On the basis of theoretical expectations of normative function (Hutchison, 1999; Kielhofner, 2002), rehabilitation professionals approach diagnostic explanations for atypicality with a value set that views normative typical performance or behaviors as desirable. These professionals therefore work with an individual to promote recovery and/or adaptation. Similar to and based on the medical explanation, the rehabilitation explanation situates the locus for atypicality primarily within an individual. While certain professions will recognize and acknowledge the effect of environmental barriers on the function of those with medical-diagnostic conditions, it remains the domain of the rehabilitation professional to assist the "impaired" individual in adapting to environmental challenges, learning behaviors, using equipment that is thought by the professional to promote "normative" function, and adapting the environment to improve function that has been limited by a diagnostic condition (Mackelprang & Salsgiver, 1999).

Consider Robert. As his hearing acuity decreased, he obtained a medical diagnosis and was referred to a rehabilitation professional educated to provide intervention related to hearing and communication impairment. The audiologist tested him, confirmed the hearing loss, and then worked with Robert to select the appropriate technological device to improve hearing. Robert was fitted with digital hearing aids and instructed by the audiologist in how to operate them.

Jennifer was referred to a physical therapist who prescribed a home exercise regimen. The occupational therapist worked with Jennifer to adapt her environment and to teach energy-saving techniques that would improve Jennifer's overall function.

Analytic Comments

To summarize, the category of medical-diagnostic explanations is comprised of two primary elements: (a) specification of the range of typical and atypical activity, appearance, and experience and (b) biomedical explanations for observations or inferences of typical and atypical. As medicine, technology, and related theory and practice have grown and expanded, the complexity of human performance has been acknowledged and considered. The acceptance of the roles that diversity patina and depth variables play in delineating, maintaining, and impeding "normal" function and appearance has grown to include gender, race, ethnicity, socioeconomic status, geographic context, spirituality, genetics, and so forth. Nevertheless, the basic tenets of normal and medical-diagnostic rationale for the abnormal comprise all the explanations in this category.

Medical explanations of atypicality have been the subject of much criticism. Several of the major objections lie in the domain of devaluation leading to limited power, control, and access in the lives of individuals with permanent diagnostic conditions (Linton, 1998).

By definition, the notion of "within normal limits," regardless of its direct use or implication through euphemism, places individuals with permanent diagnoses that result in atypicality as pathological, not normal, labeled by others on the basis of a circumscribed body of private knowledge, and subject to control and judgment. While medicine has provided significant benefit to disabled people, there are some who suggest that the mere acceptance of medical intervention with regard to prevention, remediation, or maintenance of one's disabled condition in and of itself devalues the circumstance and experience of disability and, by default, the disabled person.

Further antipathy toward the medical-diagnostic school of thought emerges from the gatekeeping function served by medical, social, and health professionals in determining access to resources and participation in activities. Some of these activities are related to the provider's domains of professional concern, and some are not.

For example, consider Marie. Her participation in public education is monitored and controlled by health providers as well as educators. In her case, the occupational and physical therapists who sit on her educational team are gatekeepers in her inclusion in educational activity as well as other school-related activities, such as team sports.

Another area of criticism is the assumed need for and unwanted imposition of formal services and professionals in the lives of disabled individuals and their families based exclusively on the presence of a diagnostic condition. As we saw with Marie, the assertion of a diagnosis often brings a host of mandated interventions that were invoked by the diagnosis of Down syndrome.

Finally, and most important, is the issue of human diversity (Schriner & Scotch, 1998). According to disability scholars, the arbitrary attribution of disability status and the concomitant devaluation to specific diagnosed medical conditions is antithetical to inclusion, civil rights, and diversity ideologies. The grand category of constructed explanations speaks primarily to this criticism.

CONSTRUCTED EXPLANATION

All the explanations that fall under this rubric explain disabling forces as relative and interactive rather than absolute physiological phenomena (Gilson & DePoy, 2002). Moreover, dissimilar to medical-diagnostic explanations, disability is attributed to external rather than internal limiting phenomena. The notion that individuals and their activities are diverse rather than fitting within categories of "normal" and "not normal" is central to this approach. Why some areas of diversity are constructed as disabilities (e.g., atypical mobility in which individuals walk with assistance) and others are not (e.g., atypical vision), despite being correctable with adaptive equipment, is a fundamental question raised by this framework.

There are numerous approaches that can be placed under the constructed umbrella. In this chapter, we limit our attention to the social, political, and cultural lenses since they encompass and represent the full scope of variables within the constructed stance. Although they overlap, there are focal differences among explanations as indicated by their names.

Whereas the medical-diagnostic explanations maintain disability as a private, internal condition, the constructed explanations have moved causes of, and thus responses to, disability into the public. These stances range from explaining atypicality as an interaction between person and environment to the large scope of disability as a civil rights issue.

We now turn to a discussion of the models that make up this explanatory category. Because the explanations overlap, we hold our critical comments until the presentation and illustration of all the explanations in this category.

Social Explanation

The social model of disability was one of the first explanatory frameworks developed in opposition to the medical-diagnostic view. As indicated by its name, to those who explain disability as a social phenomenon, medical and/or diagnostic conditions and/or diagnoses are socially interactive. While an internal condition may be acknowledged, it is not necessarily undesirable or in need of remediation (Quinn, 1998; Shakespeare & Watson, 1997). The incapacity to look or act as expected within one's social context is in large part related to a hostile environment in which barriers for participation clash against personal choice (Gleeson, 1997). Negative attitudes, limited physical access, limited access to communication and/or resources, as well as exclusion from the rights and privileges of a social group are considered just some of the barriers that interfere with the an individual's potential to actualize his or her desired roles (Barnes & Mercer, 1997). Thus, medical and diagnostic conditions are viewed as diversity of the human condition and not as an undesirable trait to be cured or fixed.

Applying this explanation to Jennifer, we can see that the cause of her incapacity to participate in public education is not her mobility atypicality but rather the physical barriers that prevent her access to the public school.

Consider Robert. Although facial scarring did not interfere with his activity, he still accepted cosmetic surgery as an intervention to normalize his appearance. Looking through a social lens, the disability would lie in the negative attitudinal responses to his atypical appearance, and the appropriate intervention might be to work toward changing cultural notions of beauty.

It is therefore not surprising that individuals with a variety of chronic or permanent explanations have advanced the social model in direct response to models that do not value the affected individual.

Individuals such as Marie and Robert, from the social stance, are disabled not by their atypical appearance or activity but rather by the devaluation that they experience within their social context. Because her medical condition is permanent, it is unlikely that Marie will ultimately engage in activity in all performance areas that fit within developmental norms. In contrast to the medical-diagnostic explanation, which would place Marie as permanently disabled as a result of her diagnostic condition, the social explanation shifts the disabling focus to a social context that, if changed, provides the opportunity for Marie to be valued, fully participatory in her community, and thus, in theory, nondisabled. Similarly, Robert would not seek treatment for scarring if his appearance were not met with social disdain.

Proponents of the social explanation of disability have further noted that discrimination can have medically and behaviorally devastating effects that provide the continuing rationale for professional domination and control over the lives of disabled individuals. Consistent with deviance theory, explicit or implicit expectations for atypicality serve to perpetuate it. The social causes of atypicality may be misinterpreted as the individual's intrinsic shortcoming, supporting the continued and even amplified need for professionally directed intervention to remediate deficits. The result is twofold: (a) benefit for the provider at the expense of the individual who is disabled by the provider's expectations and (b) continued devaluation of the disabled person. The host of professionals involved in Marie's life would provide evidence for this claim.

Because social explanations posit disability as socially constructed, the locus of the "problem" to be addressed by services and supports lies within the social context in which people interact. Rather than attempting to change or fix the person, a social explanation sets service goals as "removal or ameliora- tion of social and environmental barriers to full social, physical, career, and spiritual participation" (French, cited in Quinn, 1998, p. xx).

Let's compare and contrast the social explanation with the medical-diagnostic explanation by looking at Robert. As Robert aged, his hearing acuity decreased, and he made a decision to retire from his work on the basis of a medical-diagnostic condition. But let's rethink this scenario from a social stance. If hearing changes due to age were considered typical and acceptable, perhaps the presence of hearing aids in pharmacies, similar to the presence of reading glasses, would allow people to try them early on and make decisions about their activity independently of diagnosis and prescription. While Robert's hearing status would not be different according to the social model, the response would be, placing the responsibility for change in the social arena.

There is significant diversity among social explanations of disability. For example, some theorists suggest that negative attitudes and social discrimina- tion result from individual fear of acting or looking disabled on the part of nondisabled individuals (Hahn, 1993). Others look more broadly at purposive organizational and institutional discrimination as a means to avoid expending resources or effort that could be put to better use (Schriner & Scotch, 1998). The term "special" speaks to this issue, as disabled individuals are perceived as needing segregated and unique assistance on the basis of enforced incompe- tence rather than on their demonstrated incapacity to be contributing mem- bers of their communities (Silvers, Wasserman, & Mahowald, 1998). Yet other theorists (Longmore & Umansky, 2001; Zola, 1993) identify the moral vestiges of social discrimination of disabled people.

Joshua, for example, questioned whether he deserved the condition of multiple sclerosis because of his behavior in his youth.

Until now, we have discussed the social explanation as a negative and discriminatory experience for disabled people. However, it is interesting to note that unlike our four characters who have not always benefited from or desired disability status, other classes of individuals, those with what we named "reportable" but not observable atypical experience, are concerned with social prohibitions that prevent their classification as disabled. We discuss this issue in more detail later in this chapter. However, at this point, let's apply a social explanation to this group.

Consider, for example, people who under the medical-diagnostic model have multiple chemical sensitivity (MCS). This group is fighting for disability status in the presence of disbelief and negative attitudes toward the efficacy of the diagnostic explanation for atypical experience. The social explanation of disability in this case illuminates how questionable diagnosis intersects with negative attitudes to exclude a group from the resources that are afforded to those with socially sanctioned disabilities. Additionally, this explanation also holds the key for improving the lives of individuals in this group in that environmental changes to eliminate those substances that elicit extreme sensitivity, rather than individual remedies such as nonparticipation in public environments or even psychiatric diagnosis and treatment, would follow from a social explanation of MCS (Baker & Lipson, 2002).

As we will see in the next three chapters, those who are on the margins of disability determination but who desire it challenge the basis of legitimacy, creating a socially acceptable hierarchy of atypicality within groups who have legitimate disability status. The example of social discrimination as a basis for exclusion from disability status provides an excellent segue to the political explanation of disability.

Political Explanation

Closely aligned with the social explanation but moving into the domain of power and resources is the political explanation. From this stance, disability is explained by power differential and political jockeying for resources. Because of the hegemony of economic resources as the seat of power in the United States, privilege increases along with economic contribution and wealth and is withheld in part or in total from those who do not produce. Thus, a primary position within the political domain holds that individuals who do not partici-pate in the economy through work or other accepted forms of capital acquisi-tion are considered politically powerless since they have nothing to exchange for privilege (Albrecht, Seelman, & Bury, 2001).

Consider Joshua to illuminate this important principle. Until Joshua was able to secure a degree that led to an economically productive career, his potential for exchange and subsequent educational privilege were limited. If Joshua did not have support from his team to pursue higher education, it is not likely that he would have had the earning potential to exercise political power in his own life or the lives of others. Now that he has been given a medical explanation for his most recent atypicality, he worries about the potential loss of his work contribution and resources.

Marie's life presents an even more alarming concern from the political stance. As a result of her diagnosis, there is an assumed incompetence about her work skills. Thus, even without evidence of incapacity, Marie is excluded from competitive wages. Consequentially, she has limited exchange power, as is often the case with individuals with medical-diagnostic labels of mental retardation.

For many disabled people, the interaction of expectations for productive and social incompetence perpetuates atypicality and justifies continued exclusion. This cycle of assumed deviance, exclusion, and limited political power maintains the status quo of poverty and powerlessness in the lives of many and is identified ultimately as the primary disabling factor from the political stance. Moreover, the attribution of unemployability or noncontribution to a medically labeled deficit obfuscates political advantage and the concurrent need for social change (Wehman, 2001).

The efforts of disability activists and scholars to assert a disability identity as an oppressed and disenfranchised culture have been politically purposive and directive. Within the past two decades, significant attention in disability studies literature and scholarship has been devoted to the application of economic theory, new social theory, and political theory to the experience of disability. The range of Marxist or neo-Marxist explanations views disability as both a socially oppressed circumstance and a commodity (Bassnett, 2001).

Consider Marie. Because she is excluded from participation in a capitalist economy, she is part of a disenfranchised group. However, along with political and economic powerlessness and marginalization, individuals with mental retardation provide economic opportunity for capitalists through numerous avenues. Service provision, exploitation in sheltered employment, and products such as special education materials and so forth are all centers of capitalist advantage at the social and economic expense of people with mental retardation.

New social theory has also been used to analyze the circumstance of disabled people as an oppressed minority. According to this explanation, dominant culture both imposes its power on and marginalizes the disabled minority for economic and political advantage. Imposition of atypical classifications and devaluation create the justification for denial of civil rights and economic exploitation of this constructed minority group. Examples include the forced adherence to provider control in exchange for resources, denial of basic liberties such as choice to live or go to public school in one's own community, and so forth (Kymlica, 1995).

The disabling circumstances of each of our characters could be explained through these lenses. In his youth, Joshua was forced to comply with treatment for and monitoring of his alcohol consumption in order to obtain support for school. Marie was directed into life skills training on the basis of a label. Jennifer was denied access to public education in her community. And Robert was forced to accept a discharge from the military against his will. All could be seen as victims of oppression and exploitation as well as commodities for service providers and others who profited from the disability industry.

Of particular importance to political explanations of disability is the debate regarding the distinction between rights and privileges. According to some liberal political theorists, rights include maximum opportunity for health, welfare, and well-being. Others suggest that distributive justice is a right in which the economic and political disadvantage of disabled individuals is worthy of affirmative responses. However, conservative theorists argue that moral decisions on well-being are not the basis of rights. Rather, rights are defined as one's capacity to be autonomous and to exercise moral judgment unimpeded by the demands of others. Thus, the construct of positive rights, which includes the range of active to affirmative responses to basic human need and fairness, is conceptualized as an invasion of the right to autonomy rather than as a civil right in a liberal society.

This debate sets up significant tension between those who need positive responses, such as accommodation to maintain health and well-being, and those who argue that positive responses may infringe on the autonomy of others. For example, the consequences of public health insurance such as Medicaid and Medicare for atypical citizens is an imposed tax that theoretically violates the autonomy of those who disagree with it. Similarly, some provisions of the Americans with Disabilities Act (ADA) of 1990 (Public Law [P.L.] 101-336), such as those requiring physical access to buildings, are considered by conservative theorists as infringements on the economic and civil rights of those who are forced to bear the cost (Hutchison, 1999).

The distinction among negative and positive liberties, rights, and privileges has been a critical factor in the establishment and enactment of two political ideologies that are pivotal to how power is conceptualized and exercised between disabled and nondisabled groups. These ideologies are inclusion and self-determination (Coutinho & Repp, 1999; Sands & Wehmeyer, 1996). Both ideologies are vague, and there is much disagreement regarding the extent to which the intent and outcome of ideology in either case are positive or palliative. Inclusion as an ideology suggests that all individuals, regardless of circumstance, have contributions to make to and the civil right to be fully participatory in their communities. Self-determination as conceptualized by Gilson and DePoy (2000) is defined as the capacity to make choices and to enact one's choices. If inclusion is actualized, all citizens have the right to supports for full participation. However, this positive liberty (Hutchison, 1999) is seen by some as infringing on the negative liberties of others. For example, some parents would challenge the use of additional resources to keep Marie in public school beyond third grade.

Moreover, the extent to which inclusion is empty ideological rhetoric or the framework for civil rights is debated among scholars, policymakers, and concerned others. The term "consumer" is an excellent example as it applies to service users. While the term implies that individuals, particularly those with cognitive atypicalities, can select from an array of services, too many studies (Gilmer, DePoy, & Meehan, 2003) have demonstrated that many people do not even have the option to choose where and with whom they live.

Similarly, the potential to exercise self-determination is also a contentious issue. Skill, opportunity, and recognition of choice are the three elements that are rarely possessed in total by disabled groups, especially those who are excluded from choice because of medical explanations for acting or thinking atypically.

On another note, Stone (1986) suggests that disability status can be a privilege, considering the benefits that are afforded to members of the disabled group. Included among these are payment of Social Security Disability Insurance and even disability parking. As we discussed earlier, the effort on the part of individuals and groups to be considered disabled provides evidence that disability classification is not all negative.

In general, political explanations for atypicality share common themes regardless of which position is taken. These include power, advantage or disadvantage, entitlement or burden, economic benefit for whom, justice, rights, and fairness. In the United States and in other countries as well, these themes are important determinants of policy at multiple levels. Policy, its interpretation, and its implementation are public statements and enforcements of legitimacy. As we look at legitimacy in more detail in the following chapters, we see the themes of political explanation in constant motion. Closely aligned with and often subsuming political explanations are cultural explanations of disability. We turn to these now.

Cultural Explanation

Explaining the atypical through a cultural lens creates a collective that is typically referred to as disability culture. Although there are multiple definitions of culture, in order to understand this explanatory approach, we define culture as a circumscribed group in which members share common experiences, symbols and meanings, tacit rules, language, history, discourse, and cultural identity. In this explanation, atypicality itself is not the basis of disability (Linton, 1998). Rather, the atypicality, regardless of its visibility or alternative explanation, creates group belongingness and distinction from other groups who do not share this common identity (Mackelprang & Salsgiver, 1999).

Within this explanation, the experience of oneself as atypical intersects with issues of race, class, gender, and power differential as important determinants of the shared experiences that bind people together in a single, identifiable community of concern (Charlton, 1998; Ingstad & Whyte, 1995). We now turn to the phenomena that have been most relevant to disability cultural legitimacy.

Cultural Identity   Cultural identity comprises the set of descriptors, characteristics, and constants that one sees as belonging to him- or herself and that render one recognizable and distinct from others. These descriptors denote the differences among various cultures and serve to distinguish diverse cultures from one another. In the case of disability, the descriptors that are recognized as characteristic of all members differ according to who is observing or reporting. The debates about who is and is not a bona fide member of the disability culture and even the existence of a single culture are contentious, with proponents of this explanation suggesting that all who identify with some atypicality experience oppression and thus belong. However, the limited empirical support for disability identity (Gilson & DePoy, 2002) raises important questions about the nature of disability culture.

The literature does provide evidence of disability culture if we define culture by a unique body of arts and humanities representing the experiences and meanings of an identifiable group. An increasing body of performance and visual arts and literature depicts the experience, biography, embodiment, and thinking of disabled artists and writers. However, the degree to which this culture explains the atypical for the diversity of individuals who are considered disabled by themselves, their families, service providers, or institutional definitions is questionable. The work seems to emerge from and to hold meaning primarily for those in academic and scholarly circles.

Nevertheless, for those who explain atypicality by culture, membership in the culture bestows identity, language, and positions groups relative to one another. Let's examine each of these points more fully.

Identity   In the cultural explanation of the atypicality disability, identity is self-determined and chosen rather than imposed. Current cultural explanations have shifted disability identity from intrinsic, functional, and/or observable physically anomalous characteristics to one of reportable shared experiences that bind disabled individuals together to counter hostile attitudes emerging from anxiety occurring outside the group membership.

Language   Language is the set of symbols that describes, sorts, classifies, and provides the forum for reporting and sharing individual experience (Rogers, 1996). Classical cultural anthropology was instrumental in illuminating the role of language in defining and unifying cultures as well as excluding undesirables from cultural groups. Building on initial work about language as an essential determinant of culture are postmodernist theorists who have explored and deconstructed language not as unitary set of meanings but as a system of symbols for which multiple meanings are attributed and through which social and political ends are achieved (Derrida, 1974). Consistent with current theory of language, Linton (1998) illuminates the language about disability as a powerful tool in the definition of disability culture as well as in advancing an understanding of disabled people as marginalized and devalued by nondisabled dominant groups.

Language is an essential gatekeeper in cultures as well. Those who belong to a culture and who share the unique cultural meanings of signs and symbols have the potential to readily identify and exclude those who do not. Thus, language usage has a significant role in creating and maintaining a bond among members of a culture and assuring the rapid identification of those who do not belong. Consider the terms used by persons with disabilities, such as "crip" or "wink." These terms would be considered derogatory when used by nondisabled people to describe people with disabilities. However, when used by disabled persons among themselves, the terms not only are "allowed" but also are often symbols of pride and community.

In our previous work, we stated our concern with euphemism, and we expand it here. Along with Heumann (1993), who has noted that we have a history that is full of suggestions (often from nondisabled people) of what we should call ourselves, we raise the issue of disability labeling.

It is our contention that language is an important window into how the speaker explains atypicality and conceptualizes disability. Person-first language suggests that the term "person with a disability" is most respectful as it positions personhood before the characteristic of disability. However, as we have stated throughout this book, we do not agree that person-first language should be used exclusively. Implicit in person-first language is the medical explanation of disability. If a person is "with" a disability, then the disabling factor is located intrinsically. However, the term "disabled person" does not imply the directionality of the disablement. One may be disabled by a legitimate medical-diagnostic, social barrier, or political powerlessness explanation. We therefore suggest the use of the term "disabled" when explanations for atypicality other than medical-diagnostic ones are considered, particularly if cultural explanations are espoused.

Positioning   The proponents of cultural explanations for atypicality assert that disability is both caused and characterized by oppression, discrimination, and marginalization. Applying cultural explanations to the atypical therefore aligns disability groups with others whose civil rights have been curtailed but who have been successful in advancing civil rights movements. Cultural explanations have been important in providing analytic frameworks for social action as well as for inclusion of disability in mainstream culture. Just the growing number of disability studies programs in universities is sufficient evidence for the value of cultural explanations of the atypical in positioning disability within the multicultural and diversity discourses on university campuses.

ANALYTIC COMMENTS ON CONSTRUCTED EXPLANATIONS

As you can see, constructed explanations of the atypical have been advantageous in many arenas, including raising the esteem of those who have been medicalized, advancing civil rights and securing economic power for certain segments of atypical individuals, and creating opportunity for choice. For example, constructed explanations benefited Jennifer through producing environmental responses to improve access to public buildings. However, it is important to consider some major criticisms of this category of explanation.

First, dismissing the medical-diagnostic explanation of atypicality begs the question of how health and social services can help one make choices and engage in valued activity. Technology, medical advances, and social supports have been instrumental in changing life expectancy and in improving quality of life. The medical conditions that explain atypicality do not disappear even in the presence of social barriers.

Robert's hearing acuity has decreased no matter what constructed explanations affect his experience. And without the medical research community, he would not necessarily have a choice to change his hearing through the use of hearing aids. Similarly, Joshua can benefit greatly from the new medications that improve the symptoms of multiple sclerosis.

A second criticism is the assumption that disabled individuals are homogeneous, that they experience oppression, and that they are powerless and marginalized. We draw attention to the correlates of disability, such as poverty, that may be just as responsible for marginalization or exclusion. It is interesting to note that many of the scholars who support constructed explanations of disability often do so at conferences held in expensive hotels that they have accessed through airline travel with the aid of expensive assistive technology.

Thus, the circumstance of economic oppression is not common to all people who identify as disabled. Moreover, the efforts on the part of some groups to be legitimated as disabled reveal that there is privilege as well as negative discrimination with regard to the atypical. Positive discrimination in the form of affirmative action is also an issue that those who espouse global oppression of disabled people do not address.

We also suggest that there are significant drawbacks and limitations in the cultural discourse as well. First, who belongs to the culture is a constant source of tension and may position people with diverse conditions against one another as political advantage is sought. For example, given the diversity of medical-diagnostic explanations for atypicality within the disability community, many individuals, such as the large cohort of people with cognitive or intellectual differences, do not participate and thus are not represented in the disability rights movement (Charlton, 1998). Political power therefore is not being attained by this collective of individuals as clearly revealed in current research (Gilmer, DePoy, & Meehan, 2003; National Organization on Disability, 2000).

Similarly, people with mental illness explanations, while a large cohort, are seriously underrepresented in the disability rights movement (Charlton, 1998).

Second, placing cultural boundaries around a group creates both belongingness and symbolic incarceration. Exemplary of this phenomenon is the litany of protective legislation. Once cultures and communities are legitimated with recognition and protective legislation, these mechanisms can become seriously constraining and marginalizing. While legislation rhetorically awards the rights to full citizenship, it also creates a confining social identity by diminishing attention to the fundamental needs of people. Thus, the characteristics of atypicality that require attention may be silenced and mainstreamed, rendering people with atypicalities at a disadvantage by masking needed supports to be included in mainstream culture (Ingstad & Whyte, 1995).

Clear examples of this phenomenon involve legislation such as the Education for All Handicapped Children Act of 1975 (P.L. 94-142), the Rehabilitation Act of 1973 (P.L. 93-112), and the ADA. With the passage of such legislation, assumptions have been made that the issues of integration, access, and accommodation have been resolved. Among legislators and the general public, a perception exists that all children, regardless of disability, are fully integrated into our schools, that environmental access has been achieved, and that community living, work, and recreation are realities; the responsibility of society to afford full civil rights to all its citizens has been achieved. Even more fundamental is the implicit statement in the passage of protective legislation that the protected groups are not protected by the legislation that has been in place for all citizens.

Similarly, difference, defined as distinguishing features of groups that set groups apart from one another, creates cultural boundaries and juxtapositions, paving the way for identity. However, as noted by many critics of multiculturalism (Walzer, 1994), identity and difference, while supporting collective action, also serve to segregate and isolate (Goldberg, 1994; Walzer, 1994). Thus, diverse cultural groups with similar political agendas not only arereluctant to come together but also frequently compete with one another to achieve the same outcome: equal opportunity. As stated by Taylor (cited in Goldberg, 1994), "The capacity to name oneself in the order of thought, while significant, does not guarantee on its own the material conditions and resources, [or] the material power necessary for social flourishing and living freely" (p. 13).

SUMMARY

In this chapter, we have looked at explanations of atypicality in detail and offered criticism for thought. The two overarching explanatory categories (medical-diagnostic and constructed) provide alternative lenses through which to view atypical activity, appearance, and experience and as theoretical guidelines for legitimacy value and response.

LEGITIMACY

We devote our attention in this chapter to the clarification, exploration, and illustration of the construct of legitimacy. We introduced legitimacy as the set of differential judgments that place explanations for atypicality within or outside of disability status. Building on current literature and theory (Jost & Major, 2002), we suggest that the attribution of disability status to an individual or group is a dynamic, value-based categorization that has little to do with the atypicality but rather with judgments and beliefs about the explanations for the atypicality. Values are a major theme in many current theories of disability. In the social and minority models, for example, values are addressed primarily as they are applied to those who have already been perceived or identified themselves as disabled (Albrecht, Seelman, & Bury, 2001; Linton, 1998; Oliver, 1996a; Silvers, Wasserman, & Mahowald, 1998). According to Pfeiffer (2002), values determine the boundaries of normal and abnormal and thus set the stage for acceptable and unacceptable human difference.

Our stance is a significant departure from current models of disability in that in Explanatory Legitimacy Theory, the value element of disability precedes categorization because it is the defining element of disability. Different from conceptual models that define disability by explanation, Explanatory Legitimacy Theory asserts that disability is determined not by the explanation but by the set of beliefs, value judgments, and expectations attributed to the explanation. We are not suggesting that people or groups who are determined to be disabled do not act, look, or experience atypically or that medical, social, and/or economic factors do not influence life experience and community support. However, we see description and its explanations within the domain of human diversity. Value judgments and beliefs, on the other hand, create the acceptable limits of diversity beyond which individuals are determined to be disabled.

In concert with the tenets of Explanatory Legitimacy Theory, we define disability as a state rather than a trait not because, as asserted in current literature (Gilson & DePoy, 2002), medical or social conditions that disable individuals can change but rather because judgment and belief—the disabling factors—differ according to who is judging whom, when, and why judgments are applied and the context in which judgment made. Thus, because of differential values among individuals, theoretical perspectives and systems, and even changing values held by a single person, the definition of disability changes despite the equivalence of atypicality and the explanation for it (Jost & Major, 2002).

Let us consider Joshua for an example of how values on differential explanations influence response legitimacy. If we look at Joshua as a young man, his atypical activity (excessive alcohol consumption) was viewed by the vocational counselor as a medical-diagnostic explanation: alcoholism. This negative value-laden explanation defined Joshua as a poor risk for subsequent support, unless Joshua was able to maintain recovery and show proof of self-control (abstinence). Thus, the vocational counselor's judgment was that Joshua had a legitimate disability explained by a medical diagnosis that required a responsible response from Joshua. In the full-team meeting, an alternative explanation for Joshua's atypical activity was offered: limited opportunity and social support. Given that this explanation is beyond Joshua's control, Joshua is still seen as legitimately disabled but worthy of support for higher education.

The following example demonstrates legitimacy changes within individuals themselves. Recently, Stephen did his first skydive. As a man with atypical walking and bending explained by the medical diagnosis of a fused hip, his medical doctor suggested that he was disabled and should not jump. However, the skydive instructor, who had the same information, suggested that Stephen was not atypical of first-time skydivers. The instructor met with Stephen, and the two men decided on a plan for a tandem jump from 12,000 feet in the air. Stephen's comments after his jump illustrate the diversity of his own response to his medical explanation for his atypical movement. He indicated that he did not see himself as disabled until he had to be helped by the instructor to position his leg outside the plane. At that time, he felt disabled because of his own devaluation of the need for assistance. In essence, the explanation, as well as his perception of what was atypical, was the need for assistance, not a medical condition. For his next jump, he is preparing to move independently. Thus, to Stephen, disability was a state of being rather than a trait. The state of disability was invoked at the point where he viewed his own activity as atypical and explained by dependency. This example also highlights the differential value judgment rendered by the instructor and the physician.

The examples of Joshua and Stephen bring us to the second important part of legitimacy, namely, the role that values play in responses to disability. Legitimate disability status ranges from privilege to oppression, from arbitrary to purposive. The social and minority explanations of atypical activity, appearance, and experience identify and analyze responses to disability status as purposively or unintentionally undesirable, while conceptualizations such as that made by Stone (1986) highlight the benefits of being labeled disabled. A careful and comprehensive analysis of value is therefore warranted to prevent a simplistic, static, or essentialist (Fuchs, 2001; Jost & Major, 2002) view of disability legitimacy, and response.

Legitimacy determination and responses occur and can be examined from numerous stances. We have separated the construct into two major stances: legitimacy from without and legitimacy from within. By legitimacy from without, we mean the stance of value sets and responses from the nondisabled world, so to speak. Consistent with Netting, Kettner, and McMurtry (1998), we look at how systems comprised of domestic units, communities, and organizations define and enact legitimacy. Value assertions and responses are made with regard to many parameters in each of those system levels, including but not limited to morality, economic advantage, perception of goodness, degree of perceived control over one's circumstance, power differentials, and justice (Yzerbyt & Rogier, 2001).

Legitimacy from within encompasses the stance of individuals and groups of individuals in accepting or proclaiming their own disability status. From this stance, we examine disability identity, disability culture, self-determination, and disability studies.

These stances are not mutually exclusive. However, the perspectives and purposes of self-definition differ from those of being defined by others. Moreover, how groups perceive the positions and cohesiveness of other groups, regardless of the actual positions held by group members, is an important determinant in legitimacy of category and response (Jost & Major, 2002).

By identifying and analyzing contemporary issues, we can approach the complexity of legitimacy as clearly as possible. Table 7.1 lists the stances of disability from without and within and briefly summarizes the issues that frame

TABLE 7.1 LEGITIMACY

Disability from Without	Disability from Within
Diagnostic legitimacy	Disability identity
Educational legitimacy	Nondisability as identity—Deaf
K–12	Disability as culture
Higher education	Pedigree
Protective legislation	Self-determination
ADA	Disability studies—what is covered, who
Violence Against Women Act	should study and teach, and who should be
Abortion	included in the discussions?
Death penalty	
Eligibility criteria for work-related resources	

our subsequent discussion. Because of the complexity of legitimacy, we cannot cover the universe of issues and all the value stances. Therefore, we have chosen exemplary and current issues to illustrate the multidimensional nature of legitimacy.

As you can see by the descriptions in Table 7.1, each of the issues is relevant to what we have labeled stance from within and from without. However, as our discussion of legitimacy proceeds in the next two chapters, we highlight why we made the internal/external stance distinction and placement of each issue. We have organized our examination and analysis of disability from without first and then from within to follow the chronology of disability theory.

Much of the current literature from disability studies, as well as that describing the experience of disability from those who have accepted or asserted legitimate disability status (which we label legitimacy from within), has been created in response to the judgments, attributions, categorization, and responses to explanations for atypicality on the part of nondisabled individuals and groups. To fully understand and analyze the stance of legitimacy from within, the stances and related actions of those who created the disability category and who have determined membership legitimacy therefore need to be explicated. We now turn to the next two chapters, which discuss the stances of disability from without and disability from within.

LEGITIMACY FROM WITHOUT

In this chapter, we discuss legitimacy from the perspectives of the individuals and groups who address disability from an external stance. That is, the values and responses in this chapter reflect how disability has been defined and treated by those who do not fit disability designations. We do not intend to suggest that disabled individuals are not involved in these issues or do not render judgments from without. However, what we highlight is how the phenomenon of disability has been examined, conceptualized, valued, and addressed by groups and systems that are designed to provide care, remediation, special treatment, or gate keeping functions that influence the lives of disabled people. As we will see, some of these determinations and actions are supported by those who are the object of them and some are not.

Table 8.1 lists the issues from the external legitimacy stance that we use in this chapter.

TABLE 8.1   LEGITIMACY ISSUES FROM WITHOUT

Diagnostic legitimacy

Educational legitimacy

Protective legislation

Americans with Disabilities Act

Violence Against Women Act

Death penalty and assisted suicide

Eligibility criteria for work-related resources

DIAGNOSTIC LEGITIMACY

We begin with diagnostic legitimacy because of its centrality to the way in which atypical activity, appearance, and experiences are explained and then conceptualized as disability. Moreover, the hierarchy of diagnostic explanations in disability determination and positive and negative legitimacy responses are important driving factors in efforts to have diagnostic groups included or excluded from disability status. As we will see when we discuss issues such as the death penalty and abortion, the desirability of including some diagnostic explanations as disabling is equivocal, considering the negative and positive consequences that different contexts create.

At this point, you might be wondering what diagnostic explanatory criteria determine a legitimate disability diagnosis. Of course, there is no easy answer. The different definitions of disability as diagnostic explanation change and shift according to time and contextual factors.

There are numerous reasons for the shift. First is the role of science and technology in medicine. As a result of the advances in these fields, many conditions that had long term or permanent consequences are now not only treatable but also curable or have been eradicated.

Consider Jennifer. She would not have sustained the illness and thus the medical explanation that resulted in mobility atypicality if she had been born after the mandatory polio vaccination program had begun in the public schools.

There are numerous examples of medical-diagnostic explanations that no longer result in long-term consequences as well, such as diabetes, which can be improved by medical intervention. On the other hand, the emergence of medical-diagnostic explanations for long-term conditions is another factor that has changed diagnostic categories. HIV/AIDS is an example of a relatively new condition that has become a medical explanation for atypicality. (We return to HIV/AIDS later in this chapter since it raises important questions regarding the relative legitimacy of medical explanations and responses.)

Technology has been paramount in changing the legitimacy of diagnoses. In addition to its discovery power, technology has adaptive and assistive potential that changes the disability legitimacy of diagnoses. A contentious example is the cochlear implant. Compromised hearing is an atypicality that can usually be explained by a medical diagnosis. For some diagnostic explanations, the cochlear implant can restore hearing to people who are hard of hearing or deaf. In the next chapter, we discuss how people with atypical hearing or no hearing may differentially define themselves with regard to legitimate disability status and the issues that have been raised by technology. Here, however, we introduce the cochlear implant as an example of what some individuals may view as a technological cure.

Let's think of Robert in a related way. His age related hearing loss is a diagnostic condition that not only can be changed but, because of the large numbers of aging baby boomers, may soon not be considered an atypicality at all for particular age cohorts.

Perhaps the most germane point to our discussion of changing diagnoses is the role of culture and economics in diagnostic legitimacy. The contextual influences on diagnosis create changes in the nature of how individual diagnoses and legitimacy are conceptualized; they also create a hierarchy of worth. We look at the change in diagnoses first.

In concert with multiculturalism and the increased focus on cultural diversity patina, the influence of one's social and cultural contexts has been integrated into legitimate conceptualizations of diagnosis. Consider, for example, the change in diagnostic parameters between the International Classification of Functioning and Disability (ICIDH-2) (Ustun et al., 2002) and the International Classification of Functioning (ICF). As we indicated in Chapter 5, the ICF, the most recent version of this classification tool, defines disability as the intersection of medical condition, functional capacity, participation in activity, and environmental factors. However, past versions were restricted to medical or psychiatric illness and relatedfunctional performance.

Similarly, the diagnostic legitimacy for mental retardation shifted from the measurement of intelligence only to function and intelligence within environmental and cultural contexts. Classifications of severity based on IQ score indicated the degree to which and the nature of what a person with mental retardation could learn. Diagnosis was made by a medical or psychological professional. While diagnosis is still the domain of professionals, the current definition of mental retardation advanced by the American Association on Mental Retardation (AAMR) has shifted. Look at Box 8.1 for the most recent definition of mental retardation advanced by the AMMR.

It is interesting to note that according to the AAMR description, mental retardation is no longer considered a legitimate diagnosis but now has been shifted into a permanent functional state. Still, the label of mental retardation requires professional designation.

Consider Marie. Had she been born in 1950, the likelihood of her attendance in public school would have been very low because of the way in which mental retardation was conceptualized and met with response. However, over the past few decades, research and ideology have changed the notion of mental retardation as static to one of cognitive difference and potential capacity dependent in large part on context and resources.

We can also look at the difference in psychiatric diagnoses over the past four decades. Diagnoses have been both eliminated and added, depending on how the limits of atypicality are defined. For example, homosexuality was dropped as a diagnostic condition in 1973 from the second edition of the *Diagnostic and Statistical Manual* of the American Psychiatric Association (1973),

---

8.1   *AAMR Definition of Mental Retardation*

Mental retardation is not something you have, like blue eyes or a
bad heart. Nor is it something you are, like short or thin.
It is not a medical disorder or a mental disorder.
Mental retardation is a particular state of functioning that begins in
childhood and is characterized by limitation in both intelligence
and adaptive skills.
Mental retardation reflects the "fit" between the capabilities of
individuals and the structure and expectations of their
environment.
(AAMR, 1995–2003)

---

indicating the shift in diagnostic legitimacy in response to social, economic,
and cultural influences.

As we can see, diagnostic legitimacy shifts over time and is influenced by
many contextual factors. It is important, however, to note the commonality of
permanence or long term condition that interferes with one's typical role
expectations as the basis for medical legitimacy. This point is critical in determination of what we call the "pedigree phenomenon." We use the term "pedigree" to denote the comparative value that is ascribed to diverse diagnostic
explanations. The hierarchy of worth of conditions is important in many arenas. We discuss this concept as it applies to self-definition in the next chapter.
Here we address the valuation of conditions with regard to their worth for positive or negative legitimacy responses.

Eligibility for protection under specialized legislation and for resources
under legislated programs for disabled people in large part contributes to the
importance of and competition within the hierarchy of conditions. If we look
to history and to current diagnostic practices, values can be ascertained by attitude and response. Through an analysis of public attitude, medical provider
attitude and response, and other arenas (such as the media in which values are
reflected), it is clear that several variables affect the presence and nature of
pedigree. First, there are numerous conditions that, although named, have not
received adequate legitimacy.

Consider, for example, the diagnosis of chronic fatigue syndrome. Because it
is a new diagnosis that is primary reportable, with variable causal explanations, it
has not received wide acceptance as a pedigreed condition. Many interpretations
of chronic fatigue suggest that individuals who receive that diagnosis are just lazy.

Fibromyalgia is another diagnosis with its atypicality as primarily reportable. This diagnostic condition receives similar skepticism. Because it is often diagnosed in the absence of other observable descriptions that are consistent with medically asserted disease processes, fibromyalgia is often perceived by those within and outside of the medical community as hypochondriasis (Gilson, 2000).

A second issue in the pedigree phenomenon is the degree to which it is believed that individuals have control over their conditions and the way in which those conditions are sustained. For example, consider HIV/AIDS. Because transmission of HIV often occurs through frowned-on social activities such as intravenous drug use or unprotected intercourse with multiple sexual partners, the associated stigma renders this condition undesirable and one that is often met with a negative social attitude and response. Moreover, if condition pedigree is low or questionable and associated with disenfranchised populations such as intravenous drug users, the legitimacy response may be even more negative, given the low social worth ascribed to the social group as well as the condition.

Finally, we suggest that hierarchy is based on the observable nature of atypicality explained by a diagnosis. We can clearly see this value reflected in the public, fetishized wheelchair symbol that is used to denote disability access as well as in responses to improved access to buildings that focus on those with seated, wheeled mobility. For the most part, conditions other than wheeled mobility that may require ramped access or preferred parking are not represented symbolically. It is interesting to note, however, that as the use of canes for assisted walking becomes more prevalent and accepted as a symbol of a person using a cane has been added to some wheelchair symbols.

The distinction between physical and mental disability also plays into the hierarchy of pedigree and response. Let us turn to Marie, Jennifer, Joshua and Robert to illustrate the points presented here.

We begin with Marie. The legitimacy of Marie's determination as disabled at first seems straightforward. With the diagnostically legitimate label of Down syndrome, Marie is an individual with mental retardation. She is immediately provided with publicly funded services on the basis of her diagnosis. So according to criteria advanced within the community, organizations including medical services and resources, educational organizations, and social service agencies, Marie is legitimately disabled. The value determination about the medical explanation for her intellectual atypicality is accepted.

Similarly, Jennifer is seen as legitimate in that her diagnoses of polio and postpolio syndrome explain her atypical mobility. However, in his youth, Joshua had an equivocal medical condition. While he has a bona fide medical diagnosis of alcohol dependence, the extent to which he is believed to have control over it begets differential responses. His current explanation for atypical vision and walking is considered legitimate, as it is outside his control. And for Robert, the explanation for his visual and appearance atypicalities is not only legitimate but high on the pedigree list and unequivocal since the explanation includes injury in service to his country. At 65, however, despite his perceived need to retire because of what he explained as medically caused hearing loss, the legitimacy of the explanation may not be considered legitimately disabling in all arenas.

Now we consider the responses to each individual. For Marie, although she meets the eligibility criteria for services, she is excluded from some parts of public education after third grade. Because of her diagnosis, she is expected to be limited and thus is directed toward educational programs in which she will not develop competitive career vocational skills. If she were to follow this direction, the likelihood of her participation in the mainstream economy would be low, and she might face poverty, dependency on public support, and devaluation. Thus the response to Marie's diagnosed explanation for her atypicalities is largely a paternalistic and exclusionary one.

Jennifer does not experience the same negative responses given that wheelchair use due to a medical explanation such as polio has a seemingly desirable pedigree. She has no diagnosed or expected cognitive or mental explanation and reflects public sentiment regarding the injustice of exclusion for no fault of her own. Of course, as we saw earlier, in his youth Joshua was treated differently by providers, one who saw his condition as his own weakness and responsibility and others who suggested that the condition was a response to poor social and familial conditions. His current explanation, however, it met with positive responses since the medical-diagnostic explanation is considered beyond his control.

Interestingly, Robert was met with immediate medical responses for his atypicalities explained by injury in the military. Yet his desired response to be treated and returned to active duty was not a legitimate option. At 65, his hearing experience is met with adaptive equipment responses by the medical community but is a mere annoyance to those around him who get impatient with his request to have statements repeated. Popular cultural responses to hearing changes due to aging range from informational and supportive to joking about decline.

The issue of diagnostic legitimacy is influenced by a host of variables that are in constant flux. However, because diagnosis is most frequently the initial point at which one's legitimacy and worth are determined, it is a critical factor to continually monitor.

EDUCATIONAL LEGITIMACY

Within the past few decades, legitimacy regarding disability determination and response by educational systems has undergone significant changes. We first address public education and then follow with higher education.

Let's revisit Jennifer to illustrate changes in legitimacy value and response in public education. In her youth, Jennifer's participation in public education was not considered to be a civil right. Her mobility atypicality explained by polio was seen as her individual problem, and thus she was legitimately disabled. While Jennifer was determined to be legitimately disabled at that point, however, the school system's response was one of benign exclusion rather than provision of educational services.

Currently, inclusion ideology is reflected in legislation governing public education. As we discussed in Chapter 3, the Individuals with Disabilities Education Act (IDEA; Public Law 100-476) stipulates that public education is a civil right and further locates that right in the least-restrictive environment. While placement in general education is rhetorically most desirable, the legislation also makes provisions for alternatives, depending on individual student need and the school's capacity to fill that need (Coutinho & Repp, 1999), thereby rendering a careful analysis of legitimacy critical to understanding educational rights and practices.

Legitimacy in public education is treated primarily from a medicalized perspective. A review of educational legislation and research on inclusion reveals that disability is typically referred to by diagnostic category and the severity of one's diagnostic condition (Coutinho & Repp, 1999; McLaughlin, Schofield, & Warren, 1999). Just the term "learning disability" denotes the medical legitimacy of disability in that it is considered a diagnostic explanation for individuals who learn in atypical ways.

Statistics examining the educational placement of students with legitimate medical explanations for their atypicality are further evidence for the presence of hierarchal legitimacy in public education. Data from 1994–1997 report that those with orthopedic conditions were most legitimate in that this group experienced the largest increase in placement in general education (Coutinho & Repp, 1999). Individuals with mental retardation, behavioral disorders, and severe disabilities (most often encompassing individuals with one or more medical conditions causing extreme atypical appearance and/or activity) were most excluded from general education, suggesting that, while meeting legitimate definitions of disability, they were met with segregation.

While exclusion is rhetorically undesirable, there is significant debate about the best setting and set of services to educate children and youth with legitimate disability status. The debate ranges from the desirability of full segregation of disabled students from general education as a basis to obtain special expertise and attention to the assertion that integration is a moral right and that all students will benefit from general education and integration with the proper teacher and environmental preparation (McLaughlin et al., 1999). Perspectives are not just founded in consideration of the rights of disabled students. Some opponents of inclusion have based their argument on the belief that including students with disabilities in general education violates the rights of nondisabled students and taxpaying parents.

Consider Marie. While her inclusion in public education and competitive skill development is seen as a moral right within the inclusion paradigm and by her family, groups such as teachers and parents of nondisabled children may be concerned that Marie's inclusion is a violation of the civil rights of others. Those who do not see morality as the basis for determining legitimate responses to disability suggest that the positive right of including Marie violates the civil rights of others to their own autonomy. In this case, the argument could be made that including Marie requires action strategies and commitments by individuals who may not necessarily choose them without being forced. Thus, the tax consequences, additional effort on the part of the teacher, and the potential loss of attention to nondisabled students would be arguments in favor of legitimate exclusion based on the value determination that Marie is disabled.

We cannot leave legitimacy in public education without briefly attending to families of disabled students. Two phenomena are particularly noteworthy in that they change the nature of parenting and expectations of who in families has the right to make decisions for disabled children.

First, parents of children who are considered by schools legitimately disabled are often the advocates for their children's educational programs, asserting the right to choose and receive inclusive or special education, depending on their expectations regarding legitimate responses on the part of schools to their children's atypicality. Thus, parents must take on roles that are not typical of parenting but are not professional, either. However, despite the rhetorical support for parent participation, parents have questionable legitimacy within service systems regarding their children's education and in many arenas have to fight a system which is less than accommodating. As a consequence, when parents must necessarily act as advocates, they often end up straying from the role of being a "mom" or a "dad" to being an enforcer of the child's rights.

Second, the phenomenon of providers as parents is another role that is experienced within families with a disabled child. Once again, parenting is confounded by expanding to providers decision-making power that is typically the domain of parents.

Consider Marie again to illustrate both parenting anomalies. Even before birth, the assertion of the diagnosis of Down syndrome elicited an automatic contact from the social worker. At that point, the introduction of providers into the family was initiated and legitimized by institutional policy and practices. Moreover, we also saw that Marie's parents had to assume the role of advocate in her education. Regardless of choice, the role that parents are expected to play in a legitimately disabled child's education is codified in the formal planning processes in which teachers, rehabilitation personnel (called "related services personnel" in the schools), and other providers meet with parents to detail and document an educational plan.

Thus, we can see once again that educational legitimacy, even though it is based on a medical explanatory approach to disability, is complicated by the responses that derive from disability determination and the way in which typical roles are changed and met with responses. Of particular note is the role of distributive justice in educational legitimacy. In addition to differences in legitimacy responses based on expected learning outcome for students and on moral grounds, questions regarding who should have what types of resources and who should decide are central to educational legitimacy.

Legitimacy in higher education is based on a different set of criteria and parameters than its counterpart in public education. It is important to recognize that in the United States, higher education is considered a privilege despite the recognition that those who go on to postsecondary education are disproportionately represented among the poor.

If we look at Joshua in his youth, we can see the legitimacy response of the vocational counselor in response to Joshua's request for college support. Reluctance to provide resources for college education indicates that college is not considered a right and thus is subject to value judgments regarding the worth of the dependent individual. In Joshua's case, the unworthy status ascribed to a medical explanation for his alcohol consumption was implicit in the position taken by the vocational counselor.

The Americans with Disabilities Act of 1990 (ADA) provides the primary legislative guidelines governing the rights of disabled students in higher education. Different from IDEA, the ADA legislates the negative right of freedom from discrimination. It is therefore illegal to exclude individuals who are otherwise qualified to participate in higher education on the basis of disability. The legitimacy criteria that are inherent in the ADA therefore are relevant to legitimacy in higher education. However, there are additional considerations, only four of which we discuss here.

One legitimacy issue in higher education is the notion of reasonable accommodation (Gilson, 1996). Debates are often heated on what professors are required to do in their classrooms in order to meet the documented needs of disabled students, who is actually disabled, and who should even be in higher-education classes. Because of the rise in litigation since the passage of the ADA in 1990, legitimacy criteria and responses have been increasingly complicated in institutions of higher education. Numerous schools have created segregated advising centers for students with disabilities who assert their eligibility for accommodations through professional documentation of their disability. Thus, once again, the medical explanatory approach is hegemonous in setting legitimacy criteria. However, as expected, there is a hierarchy of legitimacy in higher education despite the theoretical notion that disabled individuals are accepted because they are qualified (Gitlow, 2001).

A second legitimacy issue is the meaning of access and accommodation (Gilson, 1996). While some institutions have operationalized these requirements through environmental access to physical spaces and the offer of additional time to complete course requirements, respectively, others have responded with broadening access to both the campus and the virtual environment and providing sophisticated technology for accommodation.

Another important issue that is especially sensitive and contentious is the legitimacy of certain medical explanations, such as learning disability and psychiatric diagnoses (Silvers, Wasserman & Mahowald, 1998). Questions regarding the existence of learning disability have emerged as students seek accommodations for atypical reading and writing (Gitlow, 2001). Similarly, the accommodation needs of students with psychiatric diagnostic explanations for atypical activity have been questioned and challenged. What is important to note here is the role of observable atypicality in delimiting legitimacy criteria in higher education. As we see, the reportable medical explanations for atypical behavior are often dismissed or distrusted as rationales for accommodation, while those in which a medical condition is clearly observable regardless of its causative role in the atypicality for which accommodation is sought are more likely to engender a positive response.

The final issue, and one that has gained much attention, is the degree to which admission criteria to institutions and academic programs in themselves are designed to exclude disabled students. Recent cases, such as that in which a blind applicant was denied admission to medical school despite his aspiration to be a psychiatrist and his assertion that with accommodation he was qualified to study in all aspects of the program (Gitlow, 2001), illuminate the role of admissions in setting the disability criteria for inclusion or exclusion. Remember that the ADA prohibits discrimination against anyone who otherwise qualifies for admission. Assertions have been made regarding the intentional stipulation of admission criteria to purposively exclude classes of protected individuals, including students with disabilities.

PROTECTIVE LEGISLATION

We mentioned the ADA earlier as legislation that prohibits discrimination based on disability. The ADA takes its place within the class of efforts that are frequently referred to as "protective legislation." We define protective legislation as that which makes it illegal to discriminate against or deny civil rights, safety, and participation on the basis of group membership. This class of legislation applies primarily to populations who have been considered legitimately discriminated against, such as ethnic and sexual minorities, again highlighting the role of value in decision making and response. In this chapter, we examine the ADA and the Violence Against Women's Act as exemplars of legitimacy issues in protective legislation.

The ADA

The ADA is protective legislation that applies to disabled individuals. Similar to other protective legislation, the ADA prohibits discrimination on the basis of disability and guarantees equal opportunity for individuals with disabilities in public accommodations, employment, transportation, state and local government services, and telecommunications. The ADA contains three introductory sections and five titles. Section 1 includes the short title and the table of contents, Section 2 details the findings and purposes of the act, and Section 3 contains definitions of auxiliary aids and services and the definition of disability. The Titles include Title I: Employment, Title II: Transportation, Title III: Public Accommodations, Title IV: Telecommunications, and Title V: Miscellaneous Provisions.

Under the ADA, disability legitimacy is comprised of a physical or mental impairment that substantially limits one or more major life activities, and the individual has a record of such an impairment or is regarded as having such an impairment. Thus, the legitimating factors constitute not only a medical explanation but also the interference of that explanation in typical and expected role behavior.

Because of the ADA's potential not only to provide opportunity where it did not exist but also to support accommodations and thus special treatment, many groups with diagnostic explanations for observable and reportable atypicality have attempted to seek coverage under the ADA. The related court cases and decisions are evidence of what we call the pedigree wars, as groups of individuals seek legitimate disability status in order to obtain rights they may feel they are otherwise denied. The questions of who should be protected and how continue to be clarified in federal courts as litigation surrounding the enforcement of the ADA proceeds.

The act stipulates that discriminatory practices, such as environmental and telecommunication barriers, need to be replaced with accessible structures in instances where cost would not be prohibitive. Thus, we see that the legitimate responses to discrimination are mediated by cost considerations. Exactly what protections are included in the act is not clear, so interpretation is subject to cultural, social, political, and economic influences as we see stated in the act itself. Recent U.S. Supreme Court decisions have favored employers over disabled individuals, reflecting the conservative political and social contexts in which these legitimacy decisions are being rendered.

Before we critically comment on protective legislation as a legitimate response to atypicality and explanations thereof, we discuss The Violence Against Women's Act (VAWA).

The VAWA, passed in 1994, states that its purpose is to protect the civil rights of victims of gender-motivated violence and to promote public safety, health, and activities affecting interstate commerce by establishing a federal civil rights cause of action for victims of crimes of violence motivated by gender. The act further clarifies the term "crime of violence motivated by gender" as "a crime of violence committed because of gender or on the basis of gender" and due, at least in part, to an animus based on the victim's gender.

Characteristic of the nature of protective legislation, the civil rights of the victims in this protected class (women) have already been asserted in the U.S. Constitution. However, additional legislation was deemed necessary to protect these rights despite existing legislation that prohibits and punishes violence and victimization of all citizens. In the most recent reauthorization of the VAWA, it was noted that subpopulations of women, including immigrants, elders, and disabled women, were continuing to experience victimization from domestic violence and sexual abuse. Legislative response has been in the form of grants to examine the phenomenon and to identify potential categorical remediation.

Because disability was not defined in the legislation, we cannot speak to the legitimacy of disability determinations in this context. However, we bring this legislation to your attention to highlight the response of legitimacy for disabled women in a service environment that was not designed to address disability per se but where exclusion has not been necessarily purposive. In essence, disproportionately high rates of abuse among disabled women continue (National Coalition Against Domestic Violence, 1996; Nosek, Howland & Young, 1997; Sobsey & Doe 1991; Walter, 1988; Young, Nosek, Howland, Chanpong, & Rintala, 1997), and abuse is often intimately associated with disability status (Gilson, Cramer, & DePoy, 2001). Thus, despite protective legislation that is layered on existing legislation, the civil rights of disabled women are still being violated in large part as a result of being perceived as illegitimate service recipients in the domestic violence system. Research has revealed that cultural attitudes and knowledge, including those held by professionals, are barriers to inclusion of disabled women in domestic violence services. For example, even though sexual assault is not considered an act of sexual passion, the myths about assault being provoked by women's sexuality is well entrenched in many social groups. Thus, because professionals often consider people with disabilities asexual, they therefore do not necessarily view sexual assault as relevant to the lives of people with disabilities (Aiello, 1986; Baladerian, 1991; Gill, 1996; Nosek et al., 1997). Moreover, despite the passage of the ADA, inaccessibility to victim services, police stations, courts, and other avenues for protection and services also are indicators of the lack of legitimacy that disabled women experience in the responses of domestic violence system.

Considering these exemplars, let us turn to a discussion of protective legislation. Central to our discussion are our assumptions that over the past 100 years, disability policy has been fragmented and poorly conceptualized (Scotch, 2001) with little recognition of the negative consequences of segregated policy responses to equal opportunity and that with the consideration, passage, and signing into law of protective legislation is the implicit message that citizens with disabilities need extraordinary protection rather than being equal under existing legislation.

We do not argue against the notion that, for many individuals with atypicalities, their experiences have been replete with instances of overt and covert discrimination and oppression. Nor do we deny that even a cursory examination of the treatment and life experiences of these individuals would demonstrate an extended history of such discrimination and oppression. However, regardless of the justification or the appropriateness of protective legislation, it is critical that we consider the impact of such legislation on the individual and the community.

As we examine federal benefit and protective legislation, it is important that we ask ourselves, To what degree might such altruistically conceived policies inadvertently or purposively serve to segregate and isolate, and is there a value to placing time limits or sundown review contingencies on benefit and protective legislation? The role of values and value conflict and change, while factored into a general analysis of policy, needs to be carefully considered in explanations about why specific subpopulations are categorically carved out to be excluded from mainstream policy, about who should be covered under extraordinary protective legislation, and about the unintended and intended consequences of conceptualization, identification, and special treatment of subpopulations.

It is within the context of the identification of subpopulations, which has been referred to as identity politics (Gilson & DePoy, 2000), that the legitimacy of the designation of disability exists. However, we raise significant concern regarding the implicit statement of failure that protective legislation asserts against legislation designed for all citizens. While we believe that the initiation of protective legislation is critically needed in order to eliminate discriminatory practices, paradoxically, its perpetuation as permanent in large part serves to segregate and continue the perception of protected groups as "special." We therefore call for a careful scrutiny of legitimacy of value and response as a basis for a full analysis of how best to craft legislation that protects the civil rights of all citizens.

The discussion of protected legislation is an excellent segue into our next legitimacy concern: the death penalty.

THE DEATH PENALTY

In this book, we do not take a position on the ethics, constitutionality, or morality of the death penalty. However, we include it here as it relates to individuals whose atypical behavior is explained by the label of mental retardation. On June 21, 2002, the Supreme Court rendered a decision making it unconstitutional to execute criminals regardless of the seriousness of their criminal behavior. The decision was justified on the basis that public sentiment had changed from support to opposition of the death penalty for individuals with mental retardation. The AAMR and others who support abolishing the death penalty for individuals with mental retardation argued that people with mental retardation are not capable of understanding all the consequences of their acts and that the death penalty is therefore excessive for those who should not be held fully responsible for their behaviors (AAMR, 1995–2003). There are many variations on this perspective, but simply stated, changing legitimacy criteria advanced by public sentiment (as supported by the number of states who have already excluded inmates with mental retardation from the death penalty) place people with mental retardation below the typical intelligence level determined as adequate for being fully responsible.

As soon as the decision was made public, opponents of this categorical exclusion argued that inmates on death row will now try to seek legitimacy as having a determination of mental retardation. The qualifier is an IQ score below 70. For death row inmates, legitimate membership in the disability category is not only desirable but also life saving.

However, on the flipside of legitimacy desirability, excusing individuals from responsibility may also be justification for excluding them from full participation in communities and social settings. Such arguments may be based on the moral paradox created by balancing right and responsibility or, even more seriously, might be the notion that individuals with mental retardation could be of potential danger to communities if they are not aware of the full range of consequences of their actions. A more fundamental question that we ask is why low IQ is a legitimate criterion for exclusion from the death penalty and other atypicalities and their explanations are not.

ABORTION AND ASSISTED SUICIDE

We include only a brief discussion of abortion and assisted suicide here to illustrate the extreme boundaries of legitimacy. Both issues are founded on similar assertions, and thus we address them together. Atypical fetal development explained by a permanent or serious medical condition such as Down syndrome has been accepted, for some, as a rationale for abortion. Similarly, disability has been accepted by many as the rationale for assisted suicide. Disability rights activists have argued that both positions imply the inhuman status placed on legitimate medical explanations and thus devalue the lives of individuals who are currently living with those explanations. Questions regarding why life can be curtailed on the basis of disability clearly challenge the presence of atypicality explained by selected medical diagnoses as a function of human diversity.

ELIGIBILITY CRITERIA FOR WORK-RELATED RESOURCES

Social Security Disability Insurance (SSDI) and Supplemental Security Income (SSI) are the two primary public sources of income for individuals who do not work. There are many Web sites and written resources that provide detailed information about eligibility specifics, application procedures, and benefits, so we do not cover them in detail here. Rather, we address legitimacy of disability status and response and provide basic overviews of these two programs for the purposes of our discussion.

The social security administration defines legitimate disability as any physical or mental problem that prevents an individual from working; the condition must be expected to last at least a year or to result in death. In order for adults to qualify for benefits under SSDI, they must meet the legitimate definition of disability and must have contributed to social security through work withholdings. (There are other ways to qualify that are related to family status as well.) Actual benefits are based on a credit system that is calculated on income and length of time that an individual has contributed to social security. Even the maximum support possible is minimal and for the most part provides subsistence-level support.

In order to receive SSI, an individual must be poor. There are several eligibility criteria for nondisabled individuals, but for disabled people to qualify on the basis of disability legitimacy, the same definition used for SSDI specifies the legitimacy criteria for disability status under SSI. The benefits received from SSI are even more meager than those provided by SSDI.

Recipients of SSI and SSDI can receive Medicaid, the health insurance program for those in poverty. Medicare (public health insurance for elders) is given to those who have received SSDI for two consecutive years. Both types of health insurance cover hospital costs, physician visits, and some other medical needs.

In order to be deemed legitimately disabled, a physician (or other specified professional, depending on the explanatory diagnosis for not working) and several other evaluators determine one's fit with the legitimacy criteria. The process is one in which an individual must prove disability legitimacy. Moreover, the rate of denial is high, after which the appeals process must be invoked if an individual still wants to seek benefits.

Until the passage of the Ticket to Work and Work Incentives Improvement Act in 1999, an individual who returned to work would lose all benefits, including health insurance. However, with this newly crafted legislation, health benefits and some income can continue as people attempt to return to work. Nevertheless, if an individual is supported on social security, it is likely that he or she will be poor.

Let us turn to an analysis of employment-related resources. As suggested by Scotch (2001), disability benefits in the United States are unemployment benefits. Scotch's claim that disability policy is actually work policy can be supported in large part by examining SSI and SSDI. Disability policy was initiated for those who had a history of contributing to the country in military service or work. In essence, this legitimacy criterion is still in operation today. Moreover, the minimal support is evidence of the devaluation of nonworking adults, even if they have a medical explanation for work atypicality. Without a medical explanation or without a work history, one may not achieve legitimacy status for SSDI. So the value on work and permanent medical diagnosis are the two criteria for disability legitimacy under social security law, and the legitimacy responses are clear. While they provide some income, those who do not work will not receive much support.

But what about health benefits? While these are most important for recipients of service, do not forget that health insurance pays providers for their work. Thus, the provision of Medicaid and Medicare, while benefiting individuals who need health care, are payment systems for those who earn.

Summary

This chapter covered a lot of ground. In looking at diverse exemplars, we can see the range of value and response elements of disability legitimacy from without. Issues such as abortion and assisted suicide raise concerns about the degree to which disabled people are valued as human, while protective legislation illuminates questions regarding the legitimacy of explanations for atypicality in civil rights and service arenas. As we proceeded in our examples, we drew your attention to important foundations that both reflect and influence values and responses. These included the presence or absence of observable atypicality, extremity of the atypicality, the legal and moral determination of rights and privileges, the dilemma of distributive justice and economic equality, and finally the economic and protective military contributions made to social institutions and communities. In all legitimacy exemplars from without, medical diagnosis (or professional documentation of an explanatory condition) is an essential legitimacy criterion. The influence of other variables such as, economic advantange values, and context intersect with medical explanations to create a hierarchy of legitimate disability status and response. As we will see in the next chapter, opposition to the medical dominance of legitimacy has been operational in legitimacy from within.

LEGITIMACY FROM WITHIN

In this chapter, we focus on how those who have been identified by themselves and/or others as disabled define disability legitimacy and response. As we indicated in the previous chapter, many responses by disabled people have been designed to counter perceived devaluation, medicalization, and oppression. However, there is a range of experiences, claimed identities, and legitimacy responses, only some of which are reactive to "without." Table 9.1 lists the issues we have selected to place alongside of our characters to provide exemplars for analysis. Although we cannot be exhaustive, we believe that these focal areas and the issues presented by our four characters represent the scope of legitimacy concerns and responses from within.

DISABILITY AS CULTURE

We begin with this topic since it is central to legitimacy definitions and issues from within. We have touched on disability culture earlier. In this chapter, we devote significant time to analysis since disability culture is an important

TABLE 9.1 SELECTED ISSUES OF DISABILITY LEGITIMACY FROM WITHIN

Disability as Culture
Disability Identity
Self Determination
Disability Studies—what is covered, who should study and teach, and who should be included in the discussions?

part of legitimacy, self-definition, and political activism. We begin with an examination of the multicultural foundation on which disability culture has anchored its thinking and actions.

Multiculturalism

Multicultural thinking grew out of a reaction to the monoculturalism of Western Eurocentrist thinking (Goldberg, 1994). Not unexpectedly, mono-culturalism eschewed the value of perspectives that deviated even minimally from the Eurocentric traditions and thus homogenized the academic and scholarly world as well as Eurocentric influence on lay culture. Moreover and critical to our discussion, economic disadvantages were experienced by those who were on the margins or outside of the dominant cultural paradigm. Assimilation into the dominant culture was therefore the sole option to exclusion (Goldberg, 1994).

In the 1960s, political and social changes shifted multicultural thought from the assimilationist to an integrationist perspective. The notion that cultures could coexist and achieve equality through integration of "others" into the mainstream was a step beyond assimilation but held mainstream, dominant culture as the ideal to which others wanted or should desire to access (Goldberg, 1994).

After the initial efforts in the 1960s, diverse debates on the nature and purpose of multiculturalism emerged and continue to be a significant part of academic rhetoric. Essentially, multicultural thought can be characterized along two ideological spectra. The first ranges from the conservative position of simple cultural description to the radical notion of multiculturalism as a political action arena in which previously oppressed cultures are posturing to gain equality not only in the economic domain but in intellectual, artistic, and other important arenas as well. The second relates to credibility in multicultural thought in provoking action, ranging from the notion of multiculturalism merely as academic rhetoric to maintain the status quo to the view of multiculturalism as capable of promoting significant social change, thereby shifting the balance of resources and intellectual power (Gilson & DePoy, 2000). A third, related ideology has emerged, that of a postcolonial gaze in which powerful cultures are seen as interlopers and exploiters of less powerful groups (Jameson & Miyoshi, 2001).

Considering the coexisting approaches to multiculturalism and the broad scope of thought that now includes postcolonialism, it is not surprising that defining multiculturalism is not an easy task. Many competing definitions and philosophical frames of reference constitute what is termed "multiculturalism." However, in examining the body of multicultural literature, four elements that are presented in Table 9.2 emerge in multicultural thinking.

TABLE 9.2

Culture exists
Pluralism
Celebration of diversity
Jockeying for power

TABLE 9.3

Exploitation—The process of taking economic or labor advantage of a group.

Marginalization—The exclusion of a group from an economic system. That group then is denied political, cultural, and economic resources as a function of nonbelongingness.

Colonialization—The imposition of culture, economic hegemony, and control over a less powerful and uninviting culture.

Powerlessness—The incapacity of a group to garner authority through which to assert its rights and privileges within a social milieu.

Cultural imperialism—The domination of multiple cultures by a powerful group and the subsequent devaluation of the beliefs and practices of nondominant groups.

Violence—The victimization of a group through attack.

First, multiculturalism is seated in the view that culture exists and is a critical part of human experience. Second, multiculturalism is founded on the notion of pluralism. That is, multiple cultures, each with its own values, practices, rituals, and meanings, are acknowledged. Third, in response to the monoculturalism of the 19th century, multiculturalism allegedly illuminates and celebrates the value of diverse cultures. Finally, the notions of domination, power, exploitation, and oppression pervade the literature on multiculturalism (Gilson & DePoy, 2000). Let's examine these constructs more fully as they relate to legitimacy.

Oppression and Exploitation

We focus mainly on oppression and exploitation since they are particularly germane to legitimacy definitions and responses. According to Young (cited in Charlton, 1998), there are five elements, or "faces," of oppression. These include exploitation, marginalization, powerlessness, cultural imperialism, and violence. Table 9.3 presents definitions of each.

In the cultural model of disability, these five elements are considered exhaustive, legitimately definitional, and in need of revolutionary response (Russell, 1998). Let's look at the lives of our four characters in the context of these terms.

Exploitation can be seen in the life of Marie. Although services are not intentionally meant to exploit her, the suggestion that she attend a sheltered workshop is an exploitive legitimacy response. As we indicated, two exploitive practices among the many that exist are prorated wages for workers with mental retardation and full wages paid to nondisabled supervisors.

Jennifer was clearly excluded from public education. Her tenacity, not civil rights, was responsible for her attainment of an advanced degree. Yet we see the potential exclusion of Jennifer from the work environment because of architectural barriers. Her experience exemplifies the marginalization to which disabled people refer.

Although we do not necessarily agree that the experience of disability is consistent with colonialization (Fanon, 1966), Robert could suggest that his surgery for cosmetic correction of facial atypicality is an example of colonialization. The rationale would be based on the imposition on Robert of a culturally hegemonous stance on how people should appear (Mitchell & Snyder, 2000). (Our challenge to the application of colonial theory to disability is seated in the degree to which the disabled community seeks to be part of the dominant culture.) Certainly, Robert has felt powerless in his life. He did not have the clout to remain enlisted in the military and thus was discharged. In addition, he was sent to rehabilitation not to pursue his own goals but to undergo remedial and cosmetic intervention necessary to participate in the economy following his retraining. Similar to the experience of colonialization, Robert might illustrate cultural imperialism by his cosmetic surgery. That is, the cultural expectation of typical appearance is so significantly imposed that people will have surgery to approximate it.

While none of the four characters has experienced violence, a significant body of inquiry has documented cultural violence in the disability community. One of the popular cultural depictions of this unfortunate circumstance is the contemporary opera *Tommy*. In its original and revival formats, *Tommy* is an opera that speaks on the surface to the disabling consequences of violence for children and the way in which continued victimization by peers and adults is perpetrated against a child who is unable to speak for himself.

From these notions of oppression and exploitation, legitimate disability cultural identity emerges. We define the general concept of cultural identity as elements that are observable or reportable and that signify belongingness. Thus, identity is comprised of descriptors, characteristics, and constants that one sees as belonging to him- or herself and that render one recognizable and unique to others (Rogers & Ritzer, 1996). Therefore, group membership and, thus, attributed group identity are determined by one's proclamation of belongingness, provided that an individual possesses the essential diversity patina and depth characteristics of the group identity and none of the exclusionary characteristics. Similarly, difference, defined as observable distinguishing features of groups that set them apart from one another, creates cultural boundaries and juxtapositions, paving the way for identity. It is therefore no wonder that disabled activists and scholars saw cultural theory as fitting and useful in uniting a critical mass of individuals.

However, as noted by many critics of multiculturalism (Walzer, 1994), identity and difference, while supporting collective action, also serve to segregate and isolate (Goldberg, 1994; Walzer, 1994). Thus, diverse cultural groups with similar political agendas not only fail to come together but also frequently compete with one another to achieve the same outcome: equal opportunity.

As we indicated in Chapter 8, many disabled people are poor, discriminated against, and often politically powerless to do much about those experiences. In response to the perceived domination that the medical field has had over determining and asserting disability legitimacy, disability studies scholars and students have shifted legitimacy explanations from medical-diagnostic to sociopolitical and cultural factors (Barnett & Scotch, 2002; Barton, 1996; Linton, 1998). The legitimately defining characteristics and experiences of disabled persons occur in the arena of political and social circumstance characterized by marginalization and oppression rather than in the observables within bodies (Garland-Thomson 1996). Thus, the cultural discourse positions devaluation, limitations in civil rights, anger, and rage as the legitimate characteristics of disability critique, dialogue, and debate (Charlton, 1998; Linton, 1998).

In many ways, it behooves disabled people to legitimately define themselves as a culture. Cultural belongingness bestows identity and language and positions groups relative to one another. Cultural belongingness bestows collective and community where such did not previously exist, and cultural belongingness distinguishes communities from one another. The Americans with Disabilities Act of 1990 (ADA; Public Law [P.L.] 101-336) and the removal of environmental barriers in Jennifer's life experience provide evidence for the positive, powerful nature of cultural identity. However, the existence of a unitary culture and the alignment with minority cultures asserted by some disability activists (Charlton, 1998; Gill, 1997; Linton, 1998) have numerous disadvantages that we address later in this chapter.

Of particular importance to disability culture is the role of language. Language is the set of symbols that describes, sorts, classifies, and provides the forum for sharing individual experience through reporting (Rogers, 1996). Classical cultural anthropology was instrumental in illuminating the role of language in defining and unifying cultures as well as excluding undesirables from cultural groups (Lévi-Strauss, 2000). Building on initial work about language as an essential determinant of culture are postmodernist theorists who have explored and deconstructed language not as unitary set of meanings but as a system of symbols for which multiple meanings are attributed and through which social and political ends are achieved (Derrida, 1974).

Language is an essential gatekeeper in cultures as well in that is an observable. For observable we do not speak here of a written language that can be seen. Rather language is an observable because it can be ascertained (though hearing, sight, and touch) by groups of people. For example, when we hear French, we typically expect that the speakers are from a "Francophone" culture (with the exception of those who speak it as a second language).

However, there is also a reportable, diversity depth element to language. Those who belong to a culture and who share the unique cultural meanings of signs and symbols—the reportables—have the potential to readily identify and exclude those who do not. Thus, language usage becomes significant in creating and maintaining a bond among members of a culture and ensuring the rapid identification, from both the stance of patina and the stance of depth, of those who do not belong.

There is much ado about language in disability studies literature as well as in the professional literature about what terms should be used to respectfully apply to disabled people as a class. We have changed our views of language and discuss several important issues about language here.

First, we assert that the concern with language is an academic one. It is a metaview on daily activity in which those of us who are privileged enough to do so examine language usage from multiple symbolic and abstract stances. We believe that the examination of language is important in disability legitimacy, provided that it is purposive. We are not specifying the purpose or dismissing the value of academic exercise. However, clarification of purpose places language and its examination in a delimited rather than an amorphous context. In asserting that disability studies literature is the language of the oppressed, we realize that many works make reference to theory that is so complex as to be inaccessible to all except those few who are conversant with the terms and concepts.

A second issue of language relates to who is speaking for whom. As we indicated in Chapter 8, professionals have created legitimacy criteria for, as well as the language to talk about, disability. The use of terms has changed from descriptors such as "cripple" or "idiot" to "individual with a disability." While we do not believe that language should be dictated or imposed, we do want to share our thinking about the term "disability" and about person-first language.

The term "disability" has been used to respectfully denote a set of circumstances as we have been discussing throughout this book. However, if we analyze the word itself, we note that the prefix "dis-" is defined as "denoting in general separation or reversal, deprive or expel from and cause to be the opposite" (Agnes, 1999, p. 517). We therefore find it interesting that those professionals who espouse inclusion use a term that has its origins in differentiation.

With regard to person-first language, we have chosen not to use it because of its implication about the circumstance of disability. The contention in person-first language (Scotch, 2001) is that the emphasis on the person should precede the emphasis on condition. But when is person-first language invoked? "Beautiful person," "black person," "nice person," "mean person," "Jewish person," and so forth are descriptive terms of people, all of which would sound ludicrous in person-first format. We are unable to find any desirable descriptors or even any conditions other than illness that are subject to person-first language. To us, then, person-first language is euphemistic at best (Heumann, 1993) and implicitly offensive at worst.

Within the concern of who speaks for whom is the notion of insider, unitary language. Among disabled people, we would suggest that there is no legitimate unitary language and no single legitimate culture or community. We turn to this point next.

To set a foundation for our position, we first discuss what we believe to be the purposes and advantages of a stance in which disability is seen as a unitary culture. Within the past two decades, the notion of "disability community" has been asserted (Gill, 1997; Gilson, Tusler, & Gill, 1997; Hahn, 1991; Longmore, 1995; Scotch, 1989). "Community" connotes an environment of acceptance and collectivity with defined roles for how community members interact, function, and act morally within that setting (Rogers, 1996) and where political, cultural, and social relationships are well identified. Social relationships are expected, and how individuals act within these roles is known and observable by the members of the community. Thus, community provides the forum for defining the typical and atypical, legitimate expectations, actions, and consequences, whereas culture provides the tacit rules and values governing that interaction as well as an ongoing narrative of human experience within diverse groups, which we refer to as diversity depth.

Communities and cultures exist in juxtaposition to one another and thus in commonality as well contradistinction. Identity and belongingness that position individuals legitimately within groups and that distinguish them include them in some arenas and exclude them from others. However, most critical to this discussion is the notion of the relative position of culture and community. Communities exist in relative position to one another in political power and resources (Gleeson, 1997; Goldberg, 1994; Kymlica, 1995) and thus compete.

As cultures change, power shifts, and struggles to maintain community position intensify (Kymlica, 1995). Contemporary disability discourse positions disability as "normal," not inferior, and demands self-determination over the resources that people with disabilities want and need (Charlton, 1998). Thus, conceptualizing disability as a single culture in which legitimacy of membership is merely an assertion is advantageous in many ways. Conceptually, the community and cultural approaches to disability legitimacy guide disabled people to draw on the experience of other marginalized groups as a basis for defining and establishing their preferred relative position.

In essence, legitimizing disability as a unitary culture places the purported disabled community into the larger narrative of multiculturalism and thus brings theory, research, and social action from multiculturalism and political theory to bear on understanding disability as an essential element of person-hood and on positioning the disability community relative to others (Ingstad & Whyte, 1995). We suggest here that identifying disability legitimately as a culture creates political advantage in order to advance the civil rights of a number of disenfranchised individuals.

Let's us look through the lens of Explanatory Legitimacy Theory to lay out the logical sequence that has brought us to our conclusions about the non-existence of disability as a singular culture. Rather than being relevant to all people with atypicalities who are classified as legitimately disabled from without, cultural legitimacy appears to be an academic and activist construct for the well-intended purpose of political, intellectual, and social growth (Gilson & DePoy, In Press). Thus, although we see many advantages of viewing disability through cultural legitimacy, we also raise significant concerns.

First, who belongs to the culture is a constant source of tension and may position people with diverse atypicalities and explanations against one another as political advantage is sought. We see this phenomenon played out in what we referred to earlier as the pedigree phenomenon. Many individuals, such as the large cohort of people with atypicality explained by mental retardation, do not participate in the cultural discourse and may not be able to access much of the disability studies literature as it is presently written. We question the extent to which cultural legitimacy excludes them and others in its develop-ment and thus is imposed on those who are unaware or unaccepting of the construct.

Second, we also see the pedigree phenomenon played out in the academic arena. Questions about who is able to write, teach, and legitimately participate in meetings about disability are debated in milieus where people with diverse atypicalities and explanations meet. For example, many individuals who assert reportable disability legitimacy express feelings of alienation and a sense of disconnection when attempting to participate in regional and national meet-ings that focus on disability.

Third, the notions of economic oppression are incongruent with the lives of disability scholars. It is difficult to resolve the cognitive dissonance that exists when a person with expensive adaptive equipment or assistive technology who has flown a great distance to speak at or participate in a conference (and stays in a fine hotel while doing so) asserts economic disenfranchisement or dis-advantage. Portraying these individuals as a legitimate part of an economically oppressed community renders hypocritical the claims of disabled identity as economically or truly socially impoverished. Thus, those who legitimately experience such dire circumstances often are dismissed by the mainstream on the basis of false claims of economic disadvantage made by individuals with atypicalities that are not explained by or met with economic oppression.

As we have indicated, placing cultural boundaries around a group creates both belongingness and symbolic incarceration. Exemplary of this phenomenon is the often well-intended protective legislation that we discussed in Chapter 8. Once cultures and communities are legitimated with recognition and protective legislation, these mechanisms can become seriously constraining and marginalizing. While legislation rhetorically awards the rights to full citizenship, it also creates a confining social identity by diminishing attention to the fundamental needs of those who it is designed to protect (Moller-Okin, 1999). We referred to examples of this phenomenon in Chapter 8, such as the Education for All Handicapped Children Act of 1975 (P. L. 94-142), the Rehabilitation Act of 1973 (P. L. 93-112), and the ADA.

While the shift to cultural legitimacy has been an important advancement in disability studies and political activism, we suggest that clarity and careful application of cultural and community stances can avoid the serious limitations of identity politics. However, we are also aware that the actual and perceived solidarity of human rights movements is essential if a critical mass of individuals is to be organized for political position (Jost & Major, 2002).

The challenge for disabled people is to keep the legitimacy dialogue open without what we are calling "dissent anxiety," which we define as a resistive and alienating response that proponents of civil rights movements express when the notion of group or cultural identity is questioned or challenged. Similar to responses to Gutmann and Appiah (1998) and Moller-Olkin (1999), each of whom questioned the scope and purpose of the overarching black and women's culture, respectively, and suggested that difference in and of itself does not equate with culture, we propose that those questions need to be asked and carefully answered, keeping in mind that legitimacy is value based and purposive. The challenge we pose through the stance of Explanatory Legitimacy Theory is for people to identify and assert legitimacy criteria that meet the ideology of self-determination. By that we mean that we support choice of both identity and cultural belonging. We discuss individual identity next and then close this chapter with a discussion of self-determination as an important stance for defining legitimacy from within.

DISABILITY IDENTITY

Disability identity has been defined in many ways. As we noted earlier, for some theorists disability identity is an asserted membership in a culture of disabled individuals who share common experiences of oppression and exclusion on the basis of public and institutional attitudes and practices toward their disabling circumstance (Gilson et al., 1997; Ingstad & Whyte, 1995; Linton, 1998). To others, disability identity is unique to individuals who have diverse explanations for atypicality. Yet others suggest the "supercrip" identity, in which disabled people prove their worth through excessive achievement.

Look at each of our characters. Jennifer both identifies as disabled and as part of a disability culture. With an atypicality from birth, she has seen the changes that have occurred as a result of disability activism and thus asserts her history of exclusion as illustrative of the circumstance of oppression and marginalization. However, Robert, Marie, and Joshua do not specify a disability identity. Although each meets disability legitimacy from without, none of the three assert their atypicality as central to who they are. Only Jennifer is aware of and reads disability studies literature.

From the cultural legitimacy stance, the concept of disability cultural identity emerged and has been espoused within disability studies (Linton, 1998). This identity is one in which the legitimate explanation of disability is located in oppression and discrimination. Thus, while a medical condition may exist, that condition is not the explanation for the disability. The benefits to individuals who identify themselves as legitimate members of a disability culture theoretically include bonding, acceptance, increased self-esteem, and political advantage. As currently conceptualized, the culture is comprised of individuals across diverse atypicalities, medical explanations, and other circumstances.

A recent study of disability cultural identity sheds an interesting light on the legitimacy of the cultural explanation of disability for 18 informants chosen for diversity patina and depth in age, ethnicity, socioeconomic status, work and/or school history, medical diagnosis, and time of onset (Gilson & DePoy, 2002). In a face-to-face semistructured interview, the informants offered a range of identity responses that were thematically analyzed and are presented in Box 9.1.

The thematic findings suggest that the legitimacy of the cultural explanation for disability is not exhaustive as claimed in the disability studies literature. Adding to and suggesting a direction for further research and clarification, the findings suggest that disability identity is distinct from disability cultural identity. Moreover, informants illustrated significant diversity in their value and their acceptance of others' values of the medical diagnoses that explained atypical activity, appearance, and/or experience. Some saw medical diagnosis as a characteristic of and explanation for disability that defined their lives, social interactions, daily activities, and future dreams, while others did not. Some attributed positive value to the disability label and experience as the forum for creating wisdom, while others devalued it as a negative, restrictive, and limiting.

The action element of legitimacy for individuals involves both response to self and response to others. As illuminated in the study findings presented in

9.1 *Thematic Findings*

Theme 1: Fitting in—The desire for acceptance in nondisabled groups to a greater or lesser degree.

Theme 2: Disability wisdom—The unique knowledge that comes from living with nontypical conditions: "I am happy that this happened to me because it has made me a better person and has made me a different person than I was. I don't know how long it would have taken me to get where I am today, and I don't consider myself financially successful. I haven't really achieved anything of great momentum to the public or to anybody, but I feel that I have gained a lot inside and have become a better person and a greater person because of it. And I don't know if that ever would have happened if I hadn't been faced with the challenges that I have been faced with."

Theme 3: It's just what you do—The continuum of approaches that respondents discussed regarding the primacy of disability in their lives, from consuming and negative to simply part of living and something that, regardless of the nature of the challenge, all people face.

Theme 4: I can do it despite what you say—The imposed label poses a challenge for "normalcy" of activity. As one informant commented, "I have been determined for a long time to become a nurse, and it is going to be a sight to be seen when I walk across the stage and get my diploma because I had to go through so much and I was determined to graduate."

Theme 5: Disability talk as shared interest versus talk as boring—The continuum of responses to conversations about their conditions and disability in general.

Box 9.1, legitimacy actions were complex. For example, the theme "I can do it despite what you say" reveals that even if an individual has negative values toward a medical explanation for atypicality, the action response to negative expectations is one of defiance through accomplishment.

On the other hand, action responses posited by Parsons (1956) in his illness model involve compliance and relinquishment of choice in exchange for services. Those who espouse the construct of disability culture demonstrate legitimacy responses of alliance and disability pride (Charlton, 1998;

Linton, 1998) to oppose what they perceive as oppressive and excluding social practices. It is important to note, however, that individual legitimacy response is not always directly reflective of one's value determination and stance. As illustrated by the theme "I can do it," such an achievement response may emerge from one's negative value on a diagnostic explanation for atypicality. The challenge met by accomplishment is therefore not necessarily an individual challenge but a social expectation of individual limitation on the basis of stereotype and stigma.

Consider Robert. His desire to continue in the military despite significant pain from being burned is in large part illustrative of this stance.

Considering the multiple influences on identity, selecting one's roles, goals, and methods to meet them is a challenge for all individuals, including people with observable and reportable atypicalities. Furthermore, we maintain that disability from within is dynamic, changing, and responsive to contextual factors. For example, while Jennifer identifies as disabled and as part of the disability culture, she does not always feel oppressed and marginalized. Her home, work, and community life have revealed contexts in which Jennifer is able to feel typical and in which explanations for her atypicality are not seen as disabilities, such as in her work as a teacher. In this role, she not only is self-determining but also provides the direction for others: her students.

SELF-DETERMINATION

"Self-determination" is a term that has been used throughout the disability studies and professional literature. However, its meaning differs according to its use and user. To some, particularly in interaction between providers and individuals with diagnostic explanations in the developmental disability category, "self-determination" is equated with a set of skills and concomitant participation in one's formal life planning. The requisite skills and planning processes are defined by professionals from an external stance in order to promote an individual's capacity to set goals and make choices on how to reach those goals (Sands & Wehmeyer, 1996). Thus, in this stance, ideology supports individual choice, but disability legitimacy remains in the professional domain.

In disability studies literature, self-determination expands beyond goal setting and planning to choosing one's identity as legitimately disabled or not. A major element of self-determination is that, in order for it to occur, recognition must be present from other groups regarding entitlement of the self-determining group not only to civil rights but also to equal opportunity and support in achieving both (Gilson, 1998).

The definition of "self-determination" as advanced here is linked to Yelaja's suggestion (cited in Hutchison, 1992) that "freedom has three components—the absence of external constraints, the ability and means to direct one's activities, and the power of conscious choice between significant, known alternatives" (p. 124). As we will see in the following examples, self-determination ideology locates legitimacy decisions and responses in the domain of the disabled individual. However, we assert that skill and knowledge are necessary in the current social, health, and service system contexts to actualize the ideology. Let us compare and contrast Jennifer, Joshua, Marie, and Robert to illustrate.

As an adult, Jennifer both has defined herself as legitimately disabled and had made choices to pursue career, marriage, and community participation. Because she held the skills to complete higher education and to live independently in the community, she set goals and pursued those goals, such as access to the workplace without professional support. Her strong identity with a disability culture was in part a response to her reading and to the advantage that she saw in the potential for political action.

Similarly, Joshua was and continues to be able to identify his goals. However, in his youth, if the vocational counselor had prevailed, it is not likely that Joshua would have acquired the education, skill, and knowledge to assume his leadership position and to now make choices about how to proceed with his most recent atypicality.

Marie, on the other hand, can be self-determining only with support from family and/or providers. She does not demonstrate the reading skill to access the disability studies literature or the knowledge and skill to advance her own goals. In Marie's case, self-determination is an interactive process as defined by Sands and Wehmeyer (1996).

Robert already sees himself as independent despite his discharge from the military and his retirement from his business. Because he does not see his atypicality through a disability lens, barriers to self-determination resulting from his atypicalities are not even on his radar screen.

SUMMARY

In this chapter, we discussed the construct of legitimacy from within. We suggested that this subcategory of legitimacy is an internal stance through which disabled people identify along the disability identity and cultural spectra, from nondisabled to disabled and from not belonging to fully belonging to disability culture. Our characters and specific issues provided points of illustration and analysis for the internal stance, and we concluded with a brief presentation of the construct of self-determination.

FASHIONING COMMUNITIES

In this section, we actualize the purpose of writing this book, the application of our theoretical lens to professional practice and social change. In the wake of the events of September 11, 2001, scholars are calling for historical criticism and contemporary theory that is both restorative and productive of social justice (Majid, 2002). Since there are no words that we could find that improve on those of Etzioni (2000), we quote his reflection and challenge as the basis of the aims of writing this book:

> Trying to sort out who has been most abusive, the most abused, who has stronger claims, will only extend the bloodshed. For now the focus should be on finding a formula that allows both [all] sides to live together. And a good way to start would be finding a way for their advocates to speak together. Sure we have reason to shout, but great reason not to. (p. B15)

In Chapter 10, we examine contemporary professional practice in rehabilitation, medicine, education, and social work and provide a formula for each to hear a full spectrum of stances from within and without as a basis for advancing professional practice and promoting social change. In Chapter 11, we illustrate how this approach, founded on the tenets of Explanatory Legitimacy Theory, through enhancing communication and logic, illuminates and has the potential to expand and shift one's stance while remaining consistent with one's values and professional scope. Chapter 12, on social justice and community, suggests that socially just communities in which diverse groups coexist must examine their categorical structures and rationales, clarify and examine the justice of the values on which these categories and responses are asserted, and be in constant axiological motion to ensure that arbitrary attribution of deviance is not the element on which decisions about need and resource distribution are based.

CHAPTER 10

THE TRADITIONAL STANCE

Putting the Cart Before the Horse

In this chapter, we briefly present, critically discuss, and illustrate the current roles and functions of several key health and social service professions and their relationships toward individuals and groups whose activity, appearance, and experience are considered atypical and explained in terms of a diagnostic category. As the chapter unfolds, the chapter's title will begin to make sense. So we leave it a mystery to be discovered as you proceed.

It is in this process of description and then explanation that health and social service professionals assert and practice the legitimization of disability. Because of the large number of professional fields that provide legitimate responses to disabled individuals, we decided to limit our discussion here to only a few of the professional fields in which disability is an important domain of concern. We realize the importance of all professions, but in the interest of both time and purpose, we selected exemplars on the basis of their broad application and on the basis of the recognition that the principles we present can be applied to health and social service professions not specifically addressed.

We also realize that the health and social service professions are diverse in their approaches to practice and research. The increasing attention to diversity patina and depth variables of culture, class, and gender (among other important influences on human behavior and experience) has been reflected in the use of multiple research methods and practice approaches (DePoy & Gitlin, 1998; Thyer, 2001). For example, nursing has been in the forefront of examining health through qualitative inquiry, in which empirical evidence relies heavily on narrative data and analysis is inductive (Morse & Fields, 1995). In this chapter, however, in order to simplify the content and focus on the principles, we discuss traditional professional practice roles as they are structured by demands for accountability and reimbursement in the formal systems that serve disabled individuals.

TRADITIONAL PROFESSIONAL STANCE

In the discussion that follows, we focus on the following areas for each profession: (a) professional scope of human activity, appearance, and/or experience; (b) problems within the profession's domain of concern; (c) legitimate explanations for disability espoused by the profession; and (d) legitimate professional responses.

Medicine

The scope of practice of medicine focuses on individual and community health and illness, diagnosis, and treatment. Within this context, the role of the physician is to collect observable and reportable information about individuals or communities and then determine whether the information fits with or deviates from the "norm" (Weitz, 2001), is considered atypical, and fits a diagnostic label. Generally, the physician bases medical explanation of atypicality on the following principles:

1. Illness is specific—Each illness has a specific set of observable and reportable atypicalities that are identifiable and that differentiate one illness from another or from nonillness.
2. Illness is universal—The manifestation of each illness will be the same across time, people, and cultures (Weitz, 2001).
3. The explanation for illness is considered to be based on a unique etiology—Specific pathology exists within the individual or is caused by unique environmental conditions, such as specific microorganisms that cause pathology.

Thus, the problem domain for physicians is pathology or illness. In the medical profession, legitimacy for the designation of disability is based on two criteria: (a) the presence of atypical activity, appearance, and/or experience explained by a diagnosis and (b) longevity of the diagnosis. The desired or preferred outcome from a medical interventive response is a return to an absence of illness or to maximum health.

The philosophical foundation of medicine lies in monism and positivism (Starr, 1982). It is assumed that the identification of atypicality (description), the pathology (explanation), determination of legitimacy (fit of diagnosis with an empirically supported long-term or permanent explanatory diagnosis), and response (as treatment) comprise a process or procedure that is based on the principles of scientific knowledge and neutrality (Weitz, 2001).

Ideally, the analysis of delimited observables and reportables results in the identification of a single diagnostic explanation for which a treatment has been determined. Table 10.1 shows the medical process in each of our characters.

TABLE 10.1	SEEING JENNIFER, MARIE, JOSHUA, AND ROBERT THROUGH A TRADITIONAL MEDICAL STANCE			
	Scope of Activity, Appearance, and/or Experience	Problems within the Profession's Domain of Concern	Legitimate Explanations for Disability Espoused by the Profession	Legitimate Professional Responses
Jennifer	Atypical musculoskeletal appearance and activity	Abnormal strength (weakness); ataxia (poor motor planning and coordination); pain	Postpolio syndrome	Rehabilitation to maintain strength and function at maximum levels; pain management through prescribed medication and activity
Marie	Atypical facial features; atypical chromosomes; reportable slowness in cognition and motor skill	Diagnosis and prognosis of permanence	Down syndrome	Referral to early intervention and rehabilitation; follow-up medical intervention as necessary
Joshua	Atypical alcohol consumption in youth; atypical vision and clumsiness in adulthood	Medical diagnosis and symptom reduction	Alcoholism in youth; multiple sclerosis in adulthood	Referral to alcohol treatment in youth; medication and rehabilitation in adulthood
Robert	Observable burns; reportable vision and hearing loss	Second- and third-degree burns and sensory loss	Limitations resulting from burns and sensory loss	Medical intervention to reduce pain, normalize appearance, and decrease scarring that limits joint motion; referral to rehabilitation; prescription for devices to improve hearing

Analytic Comments on Medicine   As we indicated earlier, and in concert with sociologists such as Conrad and Schneider (cited in Weitz, 2000) and as asserted by Pfeiffer (2002), we agree that social values affect definitions of illness, typicality, and atypicality. Moreover, many scholars assert that objectivity, defined as a bias-free process, is not possible. Just the assumption that a medical diagnosis can explain observed and/or reported phenomena is in itself a bias. Think about alternative explanations that others have used for what is often described as illness and cure. For example, religious beliefs, social conditions, and so forth are often invoked as causes and cures of conditions.

The process whereby a behavior or experience is explained as a medical problem requiring a biologically based medical response has been termed "medicalization" (Starr, 1984). This concept is especially important to legitimacy in that physicians have become decision makers ands gatekeepers in areas that are both relevant and distant from medical decision making, such as employment and even preferred parking (Bassnett, 2001; Stone, 1986).

Although using much of the same knowledge for the basis of practice as medicine, nursing differs in scope, function, and legitimacy. We now turn to a discussion of nursing in its traditional sense.

Nursing

We have separated nursing from medicine and the other professions in large part because, as a profession, the scope of nursing practice includes domains from multiple areas, including the medical profession, psychology, and social work. Although nursing has many different functions, levels of practice, and practice settings, we restrict our discussion here to the basic, entry-level nursing functions of caring for or nurturing another individual. Within this narrow scope, the focus of nursing is on the restoration and maintenance of health of the individual (American Nurses Association, 2002). Atypicality would be defined through the experience of ill health, injury, sickness, or disease. As such, this atypicality is explained as a physiological and/or psychological condition that, in concert with medical explanations, is both specific (having a unique set of signs and symptoms) and universal (an illness is manifested the same across time, people, and cultures).

Parallel to the field of medicine discussed previously and the professions of psychology and social work discussed later in this chapter, nursing is linked to the assumption that empirical observation can be applied to the activities, appearance, and experiences (symptoms or pathology) of an individual and through the use of observable and reportable assessment. Based on ascertained information, the classification of health, illness, and/or specific disease occurs through explaining relevant data with a diagnostic category specified as part of an accepted taxonomy, such as the International Classification of Disease (World Health Organization, 2001) or the *Diagnostic and Statistical Manual* (American Psychiatric Association, 2000).

The judgment regarding the nature of the classification, permanency, or long-term medical diagnosis serves as the disability legitimacy determination. In similar fashion to the practice of medicine by the physician, the desired or preferred outcome from a nursing response is a return to an absence of illness or to maximum health. Table 10.2 shows how each of our four characters meets with nursing legitimacy and response.

TABLE 10.2	SEEING JENNIFER, MARIE, JOSHUA, AND ROBERT THROUGH A TRADITIONAL NURSING STANCE			
	Scope of Activity, Appearance, and/or Experience	**Problems within the Profession's Domain of Concern**	**Legitimate Explanations for Disability Espoused by the Profession**	**Legitimate Professional Responses**
Jennifer	Atypical musculoskeletal appearance and activity	Abnormal strength (weakness); ataxia (poor motor planning and coordination); pain	Postpolio syndrome	Education about health maintenance and promotion; instruction in prescribed medication and activity
Marie	Atypical facial features; atypical chromosomes; reportable slowness in cognition and motor skill	Diagnosis and prognosis of permanence	Down syndrome	Family education in monitoring health, nutrition, and giving care; instruction in medical and care routines to promote health
Joshua	Atypical alcohol consumption in youth; atypical vision and clumsiness in adulthood	Medical diagnosis and symptom reduction	Alcoholism in youth; multiple sclerosis in adulthood	Participation in alcohol treatment in youth, including nutritional and health education; compliance instructions with medical routines and maintenance of sobriety in youth; health maintenance and promotion education, self-monitoring, medication instructions, nutrition, and care in adulthood
Robert	Observable burns; reportable vision and hearing loss	Second- and third-degree burns and sensory loss	Limitations resulting from burns and sensory loss	Burn care and education; pain reduction regimen and education; skin care for scar reduction; education in health promotion

Analytic Comments on Nursing   As you can see by reviewing Table 10.2, while nursing explanations for atypicality are based in medical explanations, the care stance shifts the locus of response to an interactive one in which, although the nurse provides services to a patient, he or she also educates patients to care for themselves and their families. Still, care, regardless of who provides it, is physiological, psychological, and nutritional and relies mainly on people taking responsibility for their own or their family's health behavior and maintenance. Most often, medical routines such as medication, nutrition, and rest constitute the scope of nursing response, be it direct or educative.

Over the past several decades, nursing has become increasingly involved in gatekeeping through case management, quality assurance, and other responses designed to organize the efficiency of provider response. In medical contexts, nurses frequently encounter disability as part of a rehabilitation team. Let's now look at rehabilitation team members.

Rehabilitation Professions

The scope of practice in rehabilitation professions is to restore, foster, or maximize function in a specified domain of professional concern (Mackelprang & Salsgiver, 1999). We use the term "function" here to reveal the normative stance of rehabilitation. That is, rehabilitation professions assume a desirable set of typical activities within age and role norms and only recently have included diversity patina and depth variables in assessment and practice. Activity, appearance, and experience outside the typical are the domain of rehabilitation.

In general, each of the professions makes a determination of what is atypical by collecting observables and reportables and analyzing them with regard to performance norms or expectations typical of an individual's age and circumstance. Rehabilitation professionals base the determination of typicality and atypicality on a model that assumes a normative pattern of human growth and development. Occupational therapists focus primarily on occupation (activity) in daily tasks and life roles (Keilhofner, 2002).

The role of physical therapists is the prevention, diagnosis, and treatment of what are identified as movement dysfunctions (atypical movement) and the general enhancement of the physical health and functional abilities of individuals (American Physical Therapy Association, 2003). Audiologists, speech-language pathologists, and speech and hearing science professionals focus their professional work toward those who have been identified as having speech, language, or hearing disorders or communication or perceptual atypicalities (American Speech-Language-Hearing Association, 1997–2002).

For each of the rehabilitation professions, the explanation for atypicality is pathology, usually within an environmental context, for which a corrective response is the development and implementation of a rehabilitation plan. In order to obtain services from rehabilitation professions, a medical referral, a self-referral, or a request for evaluation and assessment from another health or social service worker is initiated. A legitimate determination of disability, similar to medicine and nursing, is based on atypicality (usually referred to as "dysfunction" in the rehabilitation professional world) in an individual who has been given a diagnostic explanation of a long-term or permanent condition. The desired practice response outcome involves achieving the maximum assisted or unassisted typical activity.

Although many rehabilitation professions might provide service, here we look at how occupational therapy and physical therapy would approach each of our characters. Table 10.3 presents physical therapy, and Table 10.4 presents occupational therapy.

Analytic Comments on the Rehabilitation Professions   For each character, the rehabilitation response is designed to reduce atypicality, increase typicality, and, to the extent possible, normalize daily activity within some diversity parameters. Interestingly, although rehabilitation explanations for atypicality are anchored in medical-diagnostic rationales, responses do not seek to remediate diagnoses. Rather, rehabilitation responses address the descriptive elements of disability through working with individuals in that domain. Responses, whether focused on activity, appearance, and/or experience or on the context of each, is still individual, diagnostically legitimated, and subject to professional notions of normalcy. The explanation for the atypicality therefore is of primary use in determining legitimacy for categorization and eligibility for service but not in crafting the response itself.

Psychology

The scope of practice of psychology, in general, is focused on individual cognition, intellectual performance, and/or emotional behavior. Atypicality is reportable as psychiatric illness or dysfunction. The explanation for atypicality, while variable depending on the specialty practice field, is commonly identified as physiological, social, neurological, or emotional pathology—the result of an undesirable social circumstance or of dysfunctional family constellation or family communication patterns.

The legitimacy criterion for determination of disability is based on a chronic or long-term psychiatric diagnosis, most commonly noted in the American Psychiatric Association's *Diagnostic and Statistical Manual*. The desired practice response outcome is psychological stability.

Table 10.5 shows how each of our characters would be met with a psychologist's response.

Analytic Comments on Psychology   Although the legitimacy criteria for disability are seated primarily in long-term psychiatric diagnoses, psychologists

TABLE 10.3 SEEING JENNIFER, MARIE, JOSHUA, AND ROBERT THROUGH A TRADITIONAL PHYSICAL THERAPY STANCE

	Scope of Activity, Appearance, and/or Experience	Problems within the Profession's Domain of Concern	Legitimate Explanations for Disability Espoused by the Profession	Legitimate Professional Responses
Jennifer	Atypical musculoskeletal appearance and activity	Abnormal strength (weakness); ataxia (poor motor planning and coordination); pain	Postpolio syndrome	Exercises and modalities (such as whirlpool, hot packs, and massage) to maintain range of motion and strength and to function at maximum levels; pain management through prescribed exercise and modalities; ambulation and/or mobility training with and without adaptive equipment; WC measurement and instruction in its use
Marie	Atypical facial features; atypical chromosomes; reportable slowness in cognition and motor skill	Diagnosis and prognosis of permanence	Down syndrome	Early intervention to assess and treat muscle tone and motor development; exercises; stretching instruction to family
Joshua	Atypical ambulation and motor planning in adulthood	Symptom reduction and maintenance of ambulation, movement, and physical function	Multiple sclerosis in adulthood	Modalities and exercise for maintenance and improvement of physical function; pain reduction; prescription of adaptive devices for ambulation, such as canes; positioning for maximum function
Robert	Observable burns and reportable pain experience	Second- and third-degree burns and sensory loss	Limitations resulting from burns and sensory loss	Modalities, stretching, and exercise to reduce pain, normalize appearance, and decrease scarring that limits joint motion

TABLE 10.4	SEEING JENNIFER, MARIE, JOSHUA, AND ROBERT THROUGH A TRADITIONAL OCCUPATIONAL THERAPY STANCE			
	Scope of Activity, Appearance, and/or Experience	**Problems within the Profession's Domain of Concern**	**Legitimate Explanations for Disability Espoused by the Profession**	**Legitimate Professional Responses**
Jennifer	Activity atypicalities in work, self-care, and leisure	Abnormal strength (weakness); ataxia (poor motor planning and coordination); pain	Postpolio syndrome	Activities to promote maximum functioning; adaptive equipment, such as jar openers and reachers; energy-saving techniques; modifying environment for maximum function
Marie	Atypicality in cognition and motor skills and related work, play, and self-care activities	Diagnosis and prognosis of permanence	Down syndrome	Early intervention; sensory integration; positioning; play activities; instructing family in functional activity
Joshua	Atypical socialization in youth; visual and mobility atypicality in self-care, work, and leisure in adulthood	Promotion of functional social activity, self-care, work, and leisure	Alcoholism in youth; multiple sclerosis in adulthood	Group activity in alcoholism treatment program to promote self-esteem, self-reflection, and adaptive behavior in youth and functional activity, environmental adaptation, and adaptive activity in adulthood
Robert	Activity atypicality due to burns	Second- and third-degree burns and sensory loss	Limitations resulting from burns and sensory loss	Adaptive activity to reduce pain, normalize appearance, and decrease scarring that limits joint motion; environmental modification and modified garments to help with dressing

TABLE 10.5	SEEING JENNIFER, MARIE, JOSHUA, AND ROBERT THROUGH A TRADITIONAL PSYCHOLOGY STANCE			
	Scope of Activity, Appearance, and/or Experience	Problems within the Profession's Domain of Concern	Legitimate Explanations for Disability Espoused by the Profession	Legitimate Professional Responses
Jennifer	None	None	None	None
Marie	Atypical slowness in cognition	Cognitive deficit	Down syndrome	IQ and psychological testing and referral
Joshua	Atypical alcohol consumption in youth; distress related to loss in adulthood	Alcohol dependence and psychosocial dysfunction in youth; possible (exogenous) depression in adulthood	Alcoholism in youth; depression related to the onset of multiple sclerosis in adulthood	Testing; group and individual counseling related to alcohol dependence and psychosocial dysfunction in youth; assessment and counseling in adulthood
Robert	Depression related to injury, loss of work, and typicality	Psychological instability	Limitations and depression resulting from burns, pain, and sensory loss	Testing; group and individual counseling

espouse multiple theoretical stances to observe and infer atypicality and explanations. Thus, the credibility and agreement of psychiatric diagnoses are more subject to scrutiny than those that are clearly observable and consistent with the medical criteria of specificity and universality. Moreover, because responses are diverse and outcome is inferable, the accountability of responses for a category of questionable and low-pedigree disability status renders psychology less understood and less credible than medicine, nursing, and, to some extent, rehabilitation professions in determining disability legitimacy. Consider the debate regarding the credibility of mental retardation as an important example.

As we indicated previously, in our discussion of reportables, the literature reveals skepticism about the nature of mental retardation as a cognitive atypicality. Because cognition and intelligence are unobservable constructs that we have called "reportables," some have theorized that what has been considered cognitive is actually behavioral or communicative atypicality (Allen & Allen, 1995). To complicate matters, intelligence testing relies on behavioral and communication indicators of the underlying, reportable, and inferable construct of intelligence.

The conflict emerging from reportables can be seen in the facilitated communication battle (Biklen, 1990). Facilitated communication is a technique whereby people who do not speak are assisted by another person to type (Crossley, 1992). Whose communication is being typed remains the battle ground between professionals who question the capacity of people with diagnoses such as mental retardation and autism to proffer intelligible thoughts (Biklen et al., 1991).

Another layer of complication is the objection to IQ testing because of the cultural bias that is asserted to be inherent in the test items (Gould, 1996). Thus, the meaning of testing and explanations for test performance should be carefully considered within alternative explanatory paradigms.

For cognitive atypicalities and, increasingly more, for behavioral atypicalities, it is therefore not surprising that neurological and chemical-diagnostic explanations have met with increasing disability legitimacy. Moreover, medication is increasing in its legitimacy in the practice of psychology. External legitimacy limits counseling and therapy through managed care and other fiscally conservative approaches such as unequal parity in payment. Thus, the short-term responses of psychological assessment and brief therapy are favored and supported by payers over long-term psychotherapy.

Education

The primary scope of practice for educational professionals involves education and learning. This area of practice includes preschool through postsecondary education.

Public education programs, primary through high school, for children observed with atypicalities consistent with the diagnosis of intellectual or learning deficit or exhibiting atypical, disruptive behavior were first mandated under federal legislation in 1975 with the Education for All Handicapped Children Act (Public Law 94-142) and then extended to cover preschool-age children in 1968 with the passage of the Handicapped Children's Early Education Assistance Act. Both acts considered that acceptable and legitimate explanations for atypicality included individual pathology—a definable or medical, psychological, emotional, or behavioral diagnosis or a social disadvantage significant enough to consequently interfere with or delay learning.

In general, the qualifying or legitimacy criterion for the determination of disability in the educational arena has been the set of identified legislated medical-diagnostic conditional categories. Commonly, these conditions were determined by either a medical-based examination or testing by a psychologist. To some degree, legitimacy criteria in some areas, such as those for which medically specific diagnoses based on observables can be made, are clear.

However, in reportable areas with inferred explanations, such as atypical learning or behavior, there is much greater contention in terms of legitimacy. The impact of this credibility lapse is twofold. First, the resulting variability of categorization and response may allow individuals to participate in and benefit from services that, under strict or firm delimiting legitimacy guidelines, would be denied. Second, variability can also be used to exclude individuals in one locale or region who might legitimately qualify for services and/or supports in another. In general, regardless of the explanation for educational performance, the desirable outcome according to the education professional is a student's age-appropriate learning and performance on standardized and accepted assessments. Table 10.6 looks at traditional education responses to our four characters.

Analytic Comments on Education   The context of public education provides the forum for many noneducators to become involved in ideology, planning, and educational practice indirectly related and thus only reportably relevant to educational process and student academic achievement. First, by virtue of public fiscal support, K–12 education leaves the educational professional group open to significant and variable public opinion, from locations with active lay school boards to federal debates in the U. S. Congress defining how the civil right of public education will be actualized and accountable for all children and youth. In each of these contexts, the tension between and debate about inclusive versus separate education is played out with rhetorical ideology and diversity patina rather than depth, often driving educational practice for students with disabilities. It is not uncommon to see disabled children placed in regular education classrooms without specific attention to their unique learning needs (Coutinho & Repp, 1999) or sent outside their communities to school districts that are reportably able to provide a full array of supports for students with medical-diagnostic explanations for atypical learning.

At the heart of public regulation is the notion of distributive justice. Given the construct of scarcity of fiscal resources, how money is spent to support the education of disabled students is often a contentious issue. Parents, educators, school administrators, policymakers, and community members often cannot reach consensus on how resources should be divided, especially when groups compete over expenditures.

Second, educational legitimacy is similar to rehabilitation legitimacy. Educators rely primarily on medical-diagnostic legitimacy that includes psychiatric diagnosis to determine legitimate disability categorization. However, educational responses are not medical, and once again we see that the legitimacy criteria for disability status diverge from the legitimate educational response to disability determination. A resulting curiosity is that those who are determined to be legitimately disabled and thus qualify for special education responses find that their education is mandated by lesson plans developed by

TABLE 10.6	SEEING JENNIFER, MARIE, JOSHUA, AND ROBERT THROUGH A TRADITIONAL EDUCATION STANCE			
	Scope of Activity, Appearance, and/or Experience	**Problems within the Profession's Domain of Concern**	**Legitimate Explanations for Disability Espoused by the Profession**	**Legitimate Professional Responses**
Jennifer	Education in classrooms that she can enter (in her childhood)	None	Atypical mobility resulting from polio	None
Marie	Atypical slowness in cognition and learning	Cognitive and learning challenges	Down syndrome	IQ and psychological testing; individual education plans; special education and related services (e.g., physical, occupational, and speech therapy)
Joshua	Atypical alcohol consumption in youth	Aberrant behavior and truancy interfering with learning and test performance	Alcohol abuse	Referral to guidance and counseling; poor performance assessment and grades
Robert	None	None	None	None

a team dominated by medical, rehabilitation, and social service professionals rather than educators. These formally written plans (individual education plans, or IEPs) are based on predictive speculations about what students with specific diagnoses will be able to accomplish with regard to educational outcome. This team decision process, or IEP process, while seeking to ensure that students would be provided with a full range of services that might help maximize education, is a process that regularly runs the risk of leaving teachers, students, and parents as secondary in the educational decision-making process.

Finally, with regard to K–12 education, the legitimate response to disability is student specific rather than universal to environments.

In higher education, note that the legislation governing access changes from education specific to the Americans with Disabilities Act. It is thus the responsibility of the student to assert disability legitimacy through the provision of medical evidence. Because higher education is not seen as a civil right, the inclusion of students with disabilities on college campuses comes under the same jurisdiction as nondiscrimination in the workplace, community, and so forth. Unlike K–12 education, no specific fiscal resources are set aside for disability.

For the most part, disability student services are segregated from general student services, and thus there is often a "disability ghetto" on campuses. Faculty response is variable in that disabled students have only recently become an interest group in higher education. Issues such as who is "otherwise qualified" to be admitted in higher-education majors, how faculty are required to respond with accommodations, and the degree to which disability is aligned with campus diversity discourses vary significantly from campus to campus. Access to the physical and virtual environments remain fortuitous, although these issues are moving to the forefront of academic concern and discussion.

Social Work

The scope of practice of direct social work is with individuals, families, groups, and communities within the context of the social environment (Kirst-Ashman & Hull, 2001). For the policy and macropractice social worker, while practice is based on an understanding of human experience, circumstances, and needs from within the social context (Netting, Kettner, & McMurtry, 1998), the locus of practice is on legislation, administration, large systems, and policy that affect individuals, groups, and communities.

The atypical experiences that often serve to generate the need for social work services commonly involve a determination of individual distress and/or social oppression and discrimination. The initial contact with a social worker generally occurs through referral by a professional or self, an agency- or a community-sanctioned social change, and/or the identification of inadequate policy and/or legislation.

The legitimacy criteria for the determination of disability by a social worker or as the result of an interaction or set of interactions with a social worker will vary. In individual, clinical encounters supported by public and/or private health insurance, the ascription of disability legitimacy is most likely to occur in a manner common to many health practice arenas by applying a long-term chronic diagnostic explanation to a set of atypical activities, appearances, and/or experiences. As the arena of practice moves beyond the individual to the family or groups of individuals with similar constellations of atypical activity, appearance, and/or experiences, legitimacy determination is commonly made on the basis of fit with preexisting eligibility criteria. The desired outcome for direct social work response would be individual and social as well as group well-being and social justice. How that outcome is actualized is not agreed on because of the multiple theoretical stances that define it. However, similar to clinical psychology, clinical social work practice is frequently aimed at the reduction of individual, couple, and family atypicalities that are explained as symptoms of psychiatric diagnoses.

Outside clinical practice, social work plays numerous roles in disability legitimacy and response. Of particular note is the verification of legitimate status and the identification of disability resource responses for which specific categorical groups are eligible. This type of social work is usually done in agency practice, such as state human service offices and so forth.

The social worker focusing professional activity on large systems might be involved in disability legitimacy legislation, policy, and response at the local, state, and federal levels. Table 10.7 identifies how traditional social work practice would look for each character.

Analytic Comments on Social Work   Because of its large scope and multiple theoretical stances, social work is diverse in its legitimacy determination and response. Different from its historical origin, social work has in large part become the predominant profession in the mental health system and has adopted stances that rely on diagnostic criteria and clinical therapy. Thus, similar to other professions in which the legitimacy criterion is a medical or psychiatric diagnosis, the legitimate response to disability in social work does not necessarily follow with direct and observable intervention to decrease or cure the diagnosis. Social work responses also occur in the realm of identifying and garnering resources for eligible individuals. Thus, although the immediate need for resources is met, the social work response often maintains the status quo of public assistance, poverty, and marginalization of disabled people.

At the agency level, social workers participate in other service systems in applying diagnostic legitimacy criteria to verify eligibility for services and to seek referral for resource response. In these roles, the social work professional maintains the status quo by accepting, supporting, and enforcing diagnostically based legitimacy criteria and responses that maintain disabled individuals and groups in marginal positions.

Similarly, social workers who direct their professional activity to traditional macropractice have tended not to challenge medical-diagnostic legitimacy and thus craft resource responses that, while considered attentive to the needs for protection and public support, further serve to institutionalize current marginalizing approaches.

COMMENTARY AND CONCLUSIONS

In this chapter, we have addressed basic legitimacy stances of professional groups that are involved with disability. We acknowledge that there are many variations on how these professions define and respond to disability, and we have also omitted educational and research roles in which these professionals engage. However, the discussion is purposive in that, through illustrating how

TABLE 10.7   SEEING JENNIFER, MARIE, JOSHUA, AND ROBERT THROUGH A TRADITIONAL SOCIAL WORK STANCE

	Scope of Activity, Appearance, and/or Experience	Problems within the Profession's Domain of Concern	Legitimate Explanations for Disability Espoused by the Profession	Legitimate Professional Responses
Jennifer	Jennifer's response to her atypical and changing musculoskeletal activity	Loss and changing circumstance resulting in stress	Atypical mobility resulting from postpolio syndrome	Counseling
	At the macrolevel, full community access and participation	Community services and supports; policy and resource distribution; inadequacy	Community response to disability	Community organization; policy practice; eligibility for resources; referral and resource acquisition
Marie	Atypical slowness in cognition and learning	Family response to Marie's atypicality and Marie's progress in school	Down syndrome	Psychosocial assessment; participation in IEPs; family counseling
Joshua	Atypical alcohol consumption in youth; atypicality in adulthood	Social-emotional causes and consequences of alcohol dependence	Psychiatric diagnosis of alcohol dependence	Individual and group counseling
		Social-emotional causes and consequences of onset of multiple sclerosis	Multiple sclerosis	Individual and family counseling
Robert	Atypicality due to war injury; sensory loss in adulthood; aging	Job loss; social-emotional causes and consequences of injury and sensory loss	Injury resulting in burns and sensory loss and hearing loss in aging	Individual counseling; participation in resource acquisition; referral and team work with rehabilitation team; in aging, information and referral for hearing support

professions in a very general sense have approached disability, we provide the basis for comparison and contrast to the approach that we present through the lens of Explanatory Legitimacy Theory.

Our analysis of professional legitimacy suggests some important themes. For example, each profession views human activity, appearance, and experience through a specific set of explanatory lenses. Those stances emerge from research and theory and are used to identify problems and professional responses to those problems. Professional expertise has contributed to great advances and quality of life for all individuals and communities.

However, we have also identified that the dominant legitimacy criterion—medical or psychiatric diagnostic explanation—does not always explain atypicality. And while many of the professional fields focus their activity on change in the descriptive element of disability (e.g., learning, social interaction, working, and self-care), diagnostic explanations as the legitimating criterion may not always be useful in informing practice response. This is the phenomenon that we call "putting the cart before the horse."

Let's look at this principle in more detail. Each profession follows a common process beginning with assessment of the presenting issue or problem, including what it is and why it occurs. The remainder of the professional intervention is shaped on the basis of this thought process. Understanding the cause of the problem is the primary guide in identifying what is needed to resolve that problem. Once that need is determined, professional actions of goal setting, intervention, and process and outcome measurement are accomplished according to the scope, knowledge, skills, and practice guidelines for each profession. But let's look back through this chapter now to see how the process unfolds and why we might suggest that an alternative approach is necessary.

Take Robert as an example. As we looked at his history, we saw that Robert sustained a significant injury resulting in second- and third-degree burns. The physician conceptualized the problem as a diagnostic condition that required treatment, and Robert was discharged because of medical incapacity. Was the physician wrong? Yes and no. Initially, the physician looked through a causal lens of injury leading to pathology and immediate need for treatment. Certainly, that was the correct response. However, what came next was where we depart with the reasoning strategy. Once Robert was medically stable, the problem, framed as injury and disability, followed him, eliminating the possibility for his returning to the military and following his own goals. Could the problem and its causes have been revisited? Could the description of Robert's activity, appearance, and experience have been revisited? Suppose that after Robert completed his medical care and became stable, he worked with an occupational therapist to determine his current activity, appearance, and experience and the reasons for them. The therapist, perhaps rather than looking at retirement as the only option, could have explained his absence from the military through the problem lens of lack of environmental modifications needed for him to return to his military work. The locus of the cause of the problem would have shifted from the medical diagnosis to the environment. Can you see how this rethinking can open many other directions for Robert, including those that are "undisabling?" (By "undisabling," we mean the removal of a disabling factor or set of factors.)

In the next chapter, we lay out and illustrate our model for professional thinking and action through the lens of Explanatory Legitimacy Theory. We call this the EL Stance—Putting the Horse Back where it belongs. Rather than beginning with explanation, we suggest that description should be the first step in any legitimacy criterion for need. We then advance a model of problem expansion in which multiple explanations can be examined and each profession can look at the extent to which its scope, values, knowledge, and skill meet the need for change in description. The model that we suggest is designed to guide professional thinking and action so that theoretical assumptions and responses are verified as relevant and useful before they are actualized.

PROFESSIONAL STANCE THROUGH EXPLANATORY LEGITIMACY

Putting the Horse Back Where It Belongs

We have arrived at the essence of why we wrote this book: the advancement of professional and social change. In this chapter, we focus our attention on professional thinking and action through the explanatory legitimacy (EL) stance. Although we limit our discussion to disability, we suggest that the approach to professional practice that we present here is relevant to professional interaction with many people, groups, and domains.

On the basis of theoretical framework presented in this book, we anchor our model for professional thinking and action on the following heuristics of professional practice in the United States:

1. Professional thinking and action are embedded within complex social, political, economic, cultural, intellectual, and historical contexts—*We have detailed the historical and current contexts of professional thinking and action throughout this book. While a surface examination might suggest that professional action is driven by client need, we have seen that multiple influences intersect to shape diverse determinations and actions.*

2. Professional thinking and action have multiple purposes, processes, and outcomes—This principle follows from the previous one as we see professional activity embedded within an economic and political context in which competition and multiple accountabilities are often issues that drive practice decisions and even professional survival.

3. Professional thinking and action have multiple and sometimes competing audiences—*We have explored the numerous audiences from the direct care recipient to the distant pharmaceutical industry or manufacturer of adaptive equipment. Certainly, the individual who uses crutches for*

mobility has competing agendas with the durable medical equipment industry, in which profit is the primary aim of activity.

4. The current basis of professional response is value–based—*As we have seen, values form the basis of one's stance, professional choice, and even scope or purview of practice. Medical values differ from social work values, and nursing values differ from the value base of psychology. Even within professions, values are disparate and with consensus not always apparent.*

5. Value judgments determine category membership and response—This principle is at the heart of Explanatory Legitimacy Theory. As we have asserted and supported through evidence, categorical membership for disability (and for other diversity patina and depth variables) is determined by the judgments about explanations for human activity, appearance, and experience. Understanding this principle is the essence of Explanatory Legitimacy Theory.

6. Category membership forms the primary foundation for professional judgment and response—This is the principle which we seek to change. We are not suggesting that categorical membership is not informative in professional practice thinking and action. Rather, we base our EL stance on the consideration of legitimate membership as only one element of information within a complex set of thinking processes that is necessary to advance professional practice. Moreover, the basis for taxonomies is one that we assert needs vigilant scrutiny, discourse, evaluation, and change.

7. Human need can best be met by shifting the locus of legitimacy and response from categorical eligibility to individual and group need within the limits of professional and community value acceptability—*This is the second major principle that forms the EL stance. We suggest that the primary purpose of professional activity should be the improvement of experience and social justice within the diversity of people and communities. We believe that only by honest and direct discourse, debate, and negotiation can the foundation of decisions and related actions among and between groups be observable, fully analyzed, opened to honest and direct examination, and celebrated. By identifying values as the basis for decision making and response, discourse can occur at the axiological level rather than being derailed to euphemism and hidden under polemics.*

On the basis of these heuristics, we now present professional thinking and action through the EL stance. We begin by detailing the thinking and action processes that organize our approach and then compare and contrast each of our characters as they would be met with traditional and EL stance approaches. We then conclude with thoughts for further analysis.

EXPLANATORY LEGITIMACY THINKING AND ACTION
FOR PROFESSIONS

Here are the four steps of EL thinking and action. Each is discussed in the sections that follow:

1. Human description mapping
2. Clarification of professional values, scope, knowledge, and skill
3. Determination of professional fit with explanatory locus
4. Determination of action processes to meet explained need

We believe that all professional thinking and action should occur within a clarified value framework and should follow a series of logical thinking and action processes that begin with the identification of a problem or issue, proceed to identify what is needed to resolve all or part of the problem, and then systematically set goals and objectives that guide action and assessment (DePoy & Gilson, 2003). However, because this book is not intended to be a practice text per se, we refer you to DePoy and Gilson (2003) for a detailed discussion and illustration of that practice approach.

In this chapter, we limit our discussion to the thinking processes and their links to specific professional responses relevant to disability practice through the EL stance. We stop short of systematic evaluation and point you to the excellent literature for clarification of those critical elements of professional responsibility.

In order to develop this strategy, we have revised problem mapping, a tool that is identified and illustrated by DePoy and Gilson (2003). Human description mapping is a thinking process through which problems in human activities, appearances, and experiences, no matter how they are initially conceptualized, can be explained and subjected to analysis. The thinking process suggests that a problem statement is dynamic, expansive, and directional. Using the metaphor of a river, the initial problem statement is one of a rock in the riverbed. Through mapping both upstream to identify causes and downstream to identify consequences of the problem, multiple explanatory frameworks can be identified and then selected as a point of professional fit and response. By using mapping, the explanatory value basis for disability legitimacy and problem-based need become clear, and the response direction is illuminated through webs of explanation. By following the logic sequence of explanation, verification of cause and consequence and the identification of possible points of inaccurate inference and response can be revealed. Consider this example.

I pose an initial problem statement: Because I had encephalitis, I can no longer ski, and I am upset.

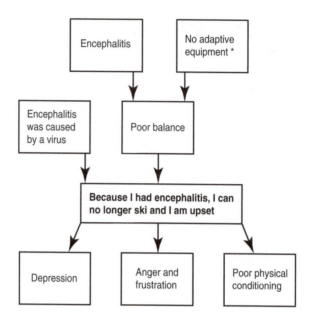

By mapping upstream, we look at causes. The encephalitis was caused by a virus (not useful for my need to ski). So we then follow another line of cause: Why can't I ski? Because my balance is poor. Why is my balance poor? Because I have cerebellar involvement from encephalitis. This explanatory line still does not get to useful explanation since the medical causes cannot be changed. However, if we ask why else my balance is poor, another explanation arises—that of no adaptive equipment. Now I have identified an explanation that I can change. Look at the visual representation above. Changing one explanatory point influences all the others and is likely to eliminate the negative consequences of not having my need met.

In the remaining three steps of the EL stance, clarification occurs in which professionals evaluate the fit of the scope of their practices with each explanation. This examination includes specification of how the profession views atypicality, the theoretical frameworks that provide the explanations for human activity, the legitimacy criteria for engaging in professional activity to address an explanation. In the previous example, a general physician may not see my recreation as the scope of professional activity or even within the value set of medicine. However, professions such as sports rehabilitation would find an excellent fit with my need and the purview of practice. The elimination of depressive consequences not only enhances life and meets my needs but also decreases cost and intervention through a simple thinking process of problem expansion and explanation.

Of course, we recognize that the practice of thinking and action is set within the context of contemporary complexity, but the clarity of the EL stance provides a solid logic sequence for analysis, discussion, and action and thus at least begins the process of legitimacy from an honest acknowledgment of value as a primary parameter in shaping decision and response.

COMPARING AND CONTRASTING TRADITIONAL AND EL STANCES

To help us with our illustration and critical comparisons, we rely on our four characters. First, we look at each as they seek assistance for a problem within an existing system. Then we rethink the process according to the EL stance and present points for thought, action, and implementation.

Let's now visit with Joshua. Because Joshua is our first volunteer, we spend a significant amount of time with him in both stances.

Joshua from a Traditional Stance

At age 45, Joshua was in the police station waiting for his wife to come and get him. He was picked up by the police at night for erratic driving, apparently called in by another driver who thought that Joshua might be drunk. When Joshua and his wife were riding home, Joshua finally described the changes he had been experiencing with his walking and vision (description of atypicality), and she disclosed to him that she feared that he was abusing alcohol again.

(Note explanatory assumption 1 from Joshua's wife: alcohol abuse)

The next day, both went to see their general physician.

(Note explanatory assumption 2: Joshua has medical illness)

The physician examined Joshua, seeking observables and reportables (including blood and urine samples), conducting a full neurological examination, and asking for a reported detailed history of Joshua's symptomology (atypicality).

(Note explanatory assumption 3: medical illness)

On the basis of these descriptions, Joshua was given an explanation of the diagnosis of multiple sclerosis. A response regimen of medication and exercise was started, and Joshua received regular medical follow-up to monitor his symptoms. The response goals for both Joshua and the physician were to make changes in the descriptive element of Joshua's life, treating the symptoms of Joshua's illness in an effort to reduce or contain them and to determine when, if ever, the intervention needed to be revised. The explanation of multiple sclerosis, while useful for prediction and guidance in medical response, has little explanatory power to guide responses to unwanted atypical activity, appearance, and/or experience.

(Note: explanatory assumption verified, goals set, and response implemented)

In efforts to address his visual atypicality, Joshua now has his wife drive him to work. He has new reading glasses that help him magnify his visual field when reading, but he still experiences double vision, for which his physician says he cannot be treated. At this point, Joshua has met the legitimacy criteria for disability membership: a medical-diagnostic label of permanence that he cannot control.

At the urging of his physician, Joshua accepted a referral to a rehabilitation team including a psychologist, an occupational therapist, a physical therapist, and a nurse. Joshua indicated that his treatment goals were to continue working and keeping his life intact. His work involves legislative and advocacy activity. Outside work, Joshua and his wife love to travel, hike, listen to music, read, and garden.

(Note explanatory assumption 4: disability resulting from multiple sclerosis)

In the team meeting, the professional staff reviewed the medical explanation of Joshua's atypicalities, and each decided to see him for an individual assessment.

The nurse saw him first, asking him questions about his daily activity and experience, including his medical regimen. She was satisfied that he was compliant with his physician's orders and felt that his observable and reportable symptoms were stable. She made plans to examine him again if he noticed any change in his atypicalities.

(Note explanatory assumption 5: disability is medically stable)

The psychologist then met with Joshua specifically to discuss his reportable, emotional experience and family dynamics. In their interaction, the psychologist asked Joshua questions about his mood, sleep, appetite, and sex drive along with eliciting a detailed report from Joshua about his daily activity and experience. On the basis of Joshua's responses indicating fatigue, less sexual activity than prior to the onset of his illness, and a desire to continue to live his life but reportable worry about the future, the psychologist suggested that Joshua speak to his physician about an antidepressant and asked Joshua to consider changing some of the activities that deplete his energy. He also felt that counseling might be indicated.

(Note explanatory assumption 6: depression related to disability)

The physical therapist saw Joshua in the clinic. In the assessment, Joshua was asked to demonstrate his strength and motor activity through performance on observable standardized testing. Scoring revealed that Joshua was below what was typical for his age and circumstance in strength and coordination.

Joshua was given strengthening and coordination exercises and instructed in how to do these throughout the day to reduce fatigue and maximize motor function. The physical therapist suggested that Joshua restrict his hiking and gardening to cool weather.

(Note explanatory assumption 7: impaired motor function and strength due to medical disability)

Through self-report and some observable demonstration, the occupational therapist assessed Joshua for his ability to engage in self-care, work, and leisure activity. On the basis of assessment findings, the occupational therapist suggested a change in Joshua's daily activity for energy conservation that he be careful to exert himself only in cool weather and that he refrain from driving unless his vision improves.

To summarize the traditional approaches to Joshua's atypicalities, Joshua expressed the goal to continue living his life without major interruption of his activity and experiences. The physician verified a medical-diagnostic explanation for the observables of atypical gait and the reportables of low vision and fatigue. This explanation fits with legitimacy criteria for disability and service response within the medical and rehabilitation service systems. Each rehabilitation professional examined Joshua in light of his or her domain of professional concern and through the explanatory lens of his or her professional knowledge. The medical rehabilitation response, based on the explanation of multiple sclerosis, includes medical monitoring; rehabilitation intervention to maximize energy, maximize strength, limit risk due to low vision, and possible prescription of mood elevators; and counseling for inferred depression resulting from loss of typical activity.

Joshua Through the EL Stance

Although the traditional explanation for Joshua's atypicality is multiple sclerosis, in looking through the EL lens, this explanation, while present and acknowledged, is not necessarily the explanation that provides the most useful guidance for professional response. Based on knowledge of multiple sclerosis as the explanatory factor, all the professionals with whom Joshua has come in contact have suggested that he change his daily activity, consider psychiatric medication and counseling, and consider restricting his recreation to specific times when the weather is cool. However, these responses are contrary in large part to Joshua's stated goals.

To begin the response process from the EL stance, the first step is human description mapping. This simple thinking process can be done by one or more people with the goal of explaining and expanding the initial problem statement. In this example, we begin with Joshua's inability to continue work unless his wife is able to drive.

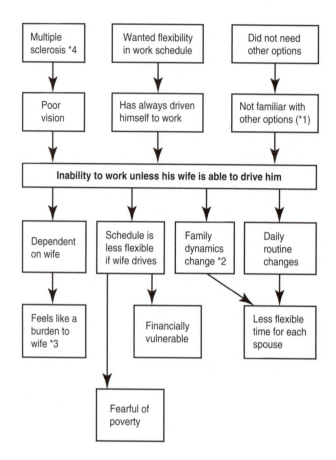

In using mapping, we would ask two questions to create a grid: "What caused the phenomenon, and what are its consequences?" As you look at the map above, notice that the initial problem is now set within the context of causes and consequences that can be verified through observables or reportables as well as those that can be targeted directly. You might further note that the traditional legitimacy criterion for professional response is no longer central as an explanatory factor. Thus, rather than focusing on the legitimacy label as the basis for defining professional response, we now look at the descriptives and their explanations in a unique life as the basis of need.

The next step involves the identification of the fit of value and scope of each professional with one or more explanations identified in the map. For example, none of the professional groups in Joshua's rehabilitation team provides transportation as part of its professional domain of concern. However, valuing independence is certainly within the domain of the rehabilitation team, and one response within the domains of several of the professionals groups (e.g., nursing and occupational therapy) would be the provision of information and problem-solving strategies to identify transportation options with Joshua. Thus, both nursing and occupational therapy might focus response on the first box in the map. But neither the nurse nor the occupational therapist would include Joshua's atypical vision in his or her scope of practice. To determine responses to this explanation, an ophthalmologist might be asked to examine need and provide more detailed explanation and response options.

If we look at the consequences of the initial problem statement, the values and scope of psychology would be consistent with the second and third boxes and might explore these with Joshua to determine the need for responses such as family counseling. The physician's role would focus primarily on the fourth box: treatment response to multiple sclerosis.

In looking at this approach, the physician, while important in responding in the medical arena, does not provide the legitimacy or the direction for need-based responses. The professionals who best fit the need with regard to values, knowledge, and skill are those who provide the legitimate response.

Jennifer Through the Traditional Stance

In her youth, Jennifer was an active child until she became seriously ill. Her parents took her to the family doctor.

(Note explanatory assumption 1: medical illness)

Following the acquisition of reportables and observables, a diagnosis of polio was made, and Jennifer was treated to the extent possible with medical intervention. As a result of the disease, Jennifer was left with a mobility atypicality.

(Note explanatory assumption 2: medical illness causes mobility atypicality)

As we noted, no legislation asserting Jennifer's right to a public education was in place in the 1950s, and thus she was educated in multiple environments, including her home.

(Note explanatory assumption 3: disability prevents education in public school)

No further professional intervention beyond medicine and nursing was provided. However, meeting Jennifer today, we see that she has sought medical advice because she is having difficulty walking with crutches, is having severe pain in her lower extremities, and reports atypical fatigue. She is having difficulty getting to work each day because of atypical mobility, weakness, pain, and fatigue.

(Note explanatory assumption 4: medical explanation is changing)

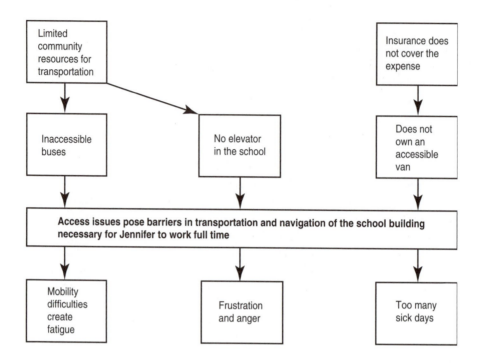

On the basis of observable and reportable information, the physician explains Jennifer's atypicalities with the diagnosis of postpolio syndrome. Responses include pain medication, prescriptions of a wheelchair and physical therapy, and a recommendation for reducing work to part-time teaching.

Jennifer Through the EL Stance

Jennifer has refused to cut back to part-time work and has consulted a social worker for assistance. Jennifer's goal is to continue to work full time as a teacher in her school system. However, access issues pose barriers for her in transportation and navigation of the school building. The social worker and Jennifer construct the human description map shown above. Note that in this map, there is no diagnosis for disability legitimacy or response. The need, according to Jennifer, is related to her atypicality but not explained by her diagnosis. In all areas of need, the social worker's values, knowledge, and skill fit with Jennifer's need, and the response is therefore to work with Jennifer and the community within the legislative rubric of the Americans with Disabilities Act to garner resources and access that will allow Jennifer to continue to work full time.

Marie from a Traditional Stance

Marie has just enrolled in third grade in her local public school. She and her parents enter the individual education plan (IEP) meeting to plan for the year.

(Note explanatory assumption 1: student with cognitive disability)

The physician, who was not in attendance but had sent notes, verified the following medical conditions: Marie has Down syndrome resulting in low muscle tone, limitations in coordination, and limitations in learning ability. The psychologist reported that Marie's low scores on the Wechsler Intelligence Scale for Children suggest that she may not be able to continue in regular education without additional educational support. The occupational therapist noted that Marie was having difficulty with dressing and self-care tasks because of her limited cognition, and the physical therapist verified the motor deficits related to Down syndrome that Marie exhibited in the playground and formal physical education classes.

(Note explanatory assumption 2: permanent diagnosis explains test scores and motor atypicality)

The IEP has outlined an educational program for Marie in which she is included in the regular classroom for history and earth science and is placed in the resource room for math and reading. In addition, she is pulled out of physical education for weekly sessions with the occupational therapist for sensory integration treatment and for postural and tone therapy with the physical therapist.

Marie from the EL stance

Marie's parents have set the goal of educating Marie in the regular classroom and therefore identify the problem statement. There are numerous points for response in the map (shown on p. 150), each within the scope, values, and fit of educational and related service professionals. Similar to Jennifer's circumstance, while the diagnostic criterion of Down syndrome is not dismissed, it is not present in the human description map, and thus medical response is not included through the EL stance to this issue. If we look at point 1, the university would provide the forum for the response of best fit. Higher education to change educational practice is the needed response for point 1. Point 2 would be best addressed by the school administration and personnel as a team. However, because the explanation of limited resources has also been identified, a systematic response, perhaps including the community, school board, and legislators, might be the most reasonable response to the complex explanation of inadequate structure and resources of the school to meet the civil rights of all students. Because the consequences of excluding Marie from the classroom are not acceptable, the school team has chosen not to address them

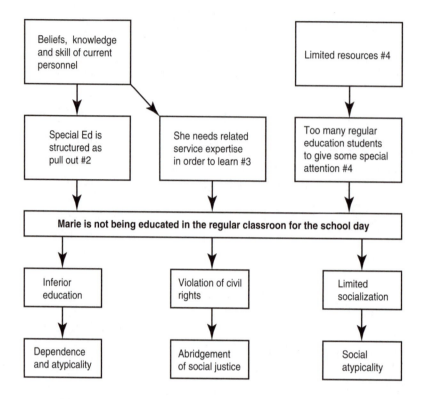

directly but, rather, to prevent them through initiating administrative, systematic, and higher-education responses.

Robert

At age 65, Robert has retired from his work and has sought medical evaluation of his hearing. The physician has sent him to the audiologist for observable information. On the basis of the findings, the audiologist diagnoses Robert with hearing loss typical of aging. According to the audiologist, Robert would benefit from the use of digital hearing aids. They are prescribed, and Robert obtains them and is instructed in their use. In this aspect of Robert's life, the traditional and EL stances are the same. The professionals who respond to Robert do so within their values, scope, knowledge, and skill.

SUMMARY AND CONCLUSIONS

We have visited with our four characters who once again assisted us in our work. We first suggested how traditional service systems and professionals might approach each individual and then looked through the EL lens to our approach for professional thinking and action processes.

We saw that the human description map is a logical thinking tool for expanding our perspectives and then laying out the areas for professional action that are need based. We suggest that this tool can be used in many arenas in addition to professional activity. For example, because of its logical foundation, mapping can be extremely valuable for social action as well as for theory testing and development and rethinking the nature of atypicality and explanations. We look at these uses in the next chapter.

What we want to highlight here is that the traditional legitimacy criteria of medical diagnosis, while useful for prediction of bodily activity, appearance, and experience, is not expansive enough to provide useful, workable explanations for the full range of human description.

Moreover, as we noted throughout and discuss in detail in our final chapter, we believe that disability legitimacy based on the medical-diagnostic explanation has a limited fit with the information needs of many professional groups who interact with disabled people. The presence of a diagnosis does not provide sufficient explanatory knowledge for human description and change and certainly does not fully illuminate how professions that do not focus on medical embodiment issues fit with legitimacy and scope.

So while medical-diagnostic explanations are useful as a shorthand language, we do not believe that the continued domination of diagnostic explanations as the basis for disability legitimacy and response provides the basis for a comprehensive approach to human need. Continued use of medical legitimacy reduces human activity, appearance, and experience to a label that is met with prescriptive response. Moreover, the value basis for legitimacy goes unspoken, along with an explication of the breadth and depth of explanatory and descriptive information necessary for sound individual responses and broad social change.

Explanatory Legitimacy Theory provides a lens and a set of systematic thinking and action processes through which description can be advanced and understood through multiple explanations for human, activity, and appearance.

A SOCIAL JUSTICE MODEL OF COMMUNITY LEGITIMACY

Robin Kelley, a biographer of social activists, reminds us to be critical for the sake of learning while keeping our vision of what should be. Throughout this book, we have presented issues and debates about the nature and experience of disability. As we moved through history, we saw the diverse contextual limits of typical and atypical, explanations for the atypical, and value determinations of worthiness criteria. From the explanatory legitimacy (EL) stance, we have analyzed disability as judgments and responses to explanations for atypicality and demonstrated how we envision professional practice through this lens. In this chapter, we follow Kelley's guidance and present our vision of community.

COMMUNITY LEGITIMACY

The EL stance provides the lens through which we envision and suggest actions to advance our ideal community. We have named this ideal "community legitimacy," denoting its theoretical and ideological foundation.

We defined the term "community" in Chapter 9, and here we add that communities are comprised of physical, social, spiritual, and environmental elements in which individuals engage in family interaction, self-care, work, leisure, citizenship, and the host of other activity categories that we have advanced in human description.

Community legitimacy is an environment in which the following values and principles inhere:

1. Equal opportunity is asserted in all areas of human description.
2. Typicality and atypicality are reframed from comparative categories to a continuum of human diversity.

3. Explanations for human description are well informed, explicit, and verified. The interests groups are therefore illuminated since who is explaining and what evidence is valued as credible are made observable.
4. Values are articulated, continuously examined, negotiated, and decided on in a democratic fashion.
5. Self-determination is seen as a right for all individuals within the value boundaries of socially just, safe communities.

We now examine each characteristic in more detail.

Equal Opportunity

As we have discussed throughout this book, legitimacy determinations and responses are based primarily on value judgments about the goodness or acceptability of explanations for human description. However, by locating response in the realm of value, we are likely to create communities, systems, and policies in which values of dominant groups serve as the basis for inclusion and exclusion.

Moreover, the discourse about response, which often is a political one, obfuscates value determinations as the driving factor in category membership and response, thus camouflaging the location where decisions are made and removing reflection and negotiation about human activity from the domain in which it belongs.

An excellent example of this phenomenon is affirmative action responses, where social change is purported to be targeted to equalizing what people can access and do in their communities. However, the locus of effort is more within what we have called diversity patina.

By placing emphasis on the observables of diversity, such as race, ethnicity, gender, age, and so forth, the assumed homogeneity of category members elicits a nomothetic set of responses as well as attributions about reportables that may or may not be accurate for group members. Thus, diversity depth based in individual experience and need may not be addressed, dialogue is limited, and social change can be averted.

From the EL stance, the first principle of community legitimacy identifies the descriptive element of humans as the essential locus of equal opportunity. We see the ideal community as one in which opportunity is based in what people want to do and experience, what people do, how they appear, and what they experience.

Let's look at Jennifer to illustrate. General attributions based in social beliefs in the 1950s, including lack of learning capability and disinterest in education on the part of children with observable atypicalities in movement, were frequently made, leading to the devaluation of universal public school access. As a result of being diagnosed with a medical explanation for an observable mobility atypicality, Jennifer was assumed not to have educational needs and was therefore denied access to her rights to public education.

This example describes what we have named community illegitimacy. In such environments, inaccurate assumptions about unrelated characteristics are made from the presence of a diversity patina characteristic. Thus, categorical labeling and related assumptions, not description, form the basis of prescribed expectation and response.

Let's look briefly at a legislative example to further illustrate. Remember that we discussed the Americans with Disabilities Act (ADA) in several chapters. Eligibility for protection under the ADA is based on explanatory medical diagnosis, not activity, appearance, and/or experience of exclusion. Thus, according to this federal legislation, disability is a categorical label based on the presence of a qualifying explanatory circumstance. The presence of the category, not the experience of discrimination related to atypicality, qualifies people for protection under the ADA. It is therefore not uncommon to see individuals clamoring to seek a diagnostic label in order to be considered part of the protected class of citizens who benefit from the ADA. Consider the large number of lawsuits that have sought damages for denial of ADA rights for specific diagnostic categorical groups.

Two additional points relevant to community legitimacy are critical here. First, if denial of civil rights on the basis of disability category membership were not experienced by many individuals with atypicalities, the ADA would not have been necessary. For us, the ideal legitimate community would apply constitutional rights and existing legislation fairly to everyone so that additional layers of law would not have to be instituted to assert the rights that already exist for all citizens. However, in light categorical discrimination, the interim use of protective legislation is reasonable.

Second, our vision of protective legislation is temporary and fashioned through the EL stance. In this scenario, categorically based legislation would be replaced with legislation that provides protection for people who have experienced discrimination on the basis of inaccurate attribution and prejudice. Although it would be likely that the same groups who are currently covered under protected categorical civil rights legislation would constitute a large majority of those who would seek justice under a law broadened to address human experience, the EL approach to interim protective legislation would not, by design, invoke the competition, conflict, separation, and exclusion of identity politics.

Typicality and Atypicality

This principle is central to our vision of community legitimacy. As we discussed in significant detail, typicality and atypicality are contextual and changeable and serve to position people relative to one another as well as to a norm. Davis

(2002) has suggested that the construct of norm be replaced with ideal. By making this conceptual substitution, Davis claims that because no one can attain the ideal, all people would be equal in their imperfection.

While we share Davis's concern about the marginalization of those who fall outside the norm, we do not agree with his assertion of equality of imperfection. Rather, we concur with Hanson (2002), who reveals the myth of categorical approaches to many variables. Her concerns focus primarily on race, age, and gender, which she asserts are continuous and in some instances arbitrary. Take gender, for example. Hanson suggests that despite the presence of sexual characteristics that have been traditional indicators of male and female, what demonstrates the continuous nature of gender are the presence of female and male hormones in all people, the size and variable function of genitalia and sex organs, and the environmental influences on gender maturation. Moreover, the addition of new genders such as gay/lesbian/bisexual/transvestite to the previous dichotomous concept is further evidence of gender as continuous.

We apply Hanson's argument to typicality and atypicality. By taking the stance that humans are diverse, the need to locate people in one or another category is eliminated. Thus, in our vision of community legitimacy, no one is abnormal, disabled, or described by any of the terms that are euphemistic for undesirable. Descriptors of activity, appearance, and experience can therefore be awarded and celebrated. From the EL stance, no one is too old, too disabled, too dumb, and so forth since the word "too" implies that one has exceeded a desirable range.

Consider walking. In a legitimate community, walking would be viewed as one method of mobility, among many others, including the use of a wheelchair, crutches. and other assistive options. This expanded notion of mobility as diverse would then translate into architecture to meet the diversity of mobility methods rather than rendering full access only to those who fit typical mobility expectations.

Explanations for Human Description

In our ideal community, the pluralism of explanatory frameworks for human activity, appearance, and experience would be acknowledged and celebrated as a beautiful, creative, and useful element of the diversity of human thinking and stance. Diverse explanations for human description not only provide the forum for rich intellectual exchange but also advance the evidence of the multiplicity of stances that inform human lives.

However, we add an additional requirement beyond acknowledgment to the ideal role of pluralistic explanations in a legitimate communities. Because explanations form the foundation for legitimacy judgment and response, they can be used as intended or unintended rationales for prejudice, denial of civil rights, community exclusion, and personal harm.

By now you may have guessed that in our vision, the legitimate community would be comprised of individuals and groups who seek explanation from those whose activities, appearance, and experiences are being explained, who specify explanatory schemes, and who verify the fit of all initially advanced explanatory frameworks with human description.

In Chapter 11, we provided and illustrated a tool—human description mapping—for each of these purposes. This approach to explanation is not limited to professional-client interaction. Rather, we see mapping and subsequent verification of cause and consequence as essential to socially just community interactions at all levels. Moreover, what evidence is purposive and accepted as credible by and useful to diverse groups is an important part of discussions regarding explanations.

Consider the contemporary trend asserting the necessity of evidence-based practice in health care. Dissimilar from what was the case several decades ago, empirically generated evidence for practice decisions, expected outcomes, and demonstrated outcomes has become central to professional discourse and now has been increasingly reflected in popular culture. But what is meant by empiricism and who understands its presentation is variable. Consider the frequent appearances of percentages and other statistical assertions in popular media, such as newspapers and news broadcasts. Typically, these numbers are not accompanied by any discussion of how those percentages were attained. Thus, while numeric evidence is presented, its meaning cannot be understood. In our vision, evidence to support the efficacy of explanatory frameworks for human description would be clear, accessible, and informative to all who are affected by and concerned with it. The limitations of the empirical report of numbers would also be included so that all who consume the knowledge can think of its value and application.

Consider this example. Disability parking is considered by many to be a privilege. It is often granted on the basis of a legitimate diagnostic disability explanation rather than on evidence of descriptive need. Thus, many people with qualifying labels but without the evidence to indicate that remote parking would be an access obstacle often sport disability parking placards. In a legitimate community, credible evidence of need would determine a disability parking response.

Values

Because of its structure, Explanatory Legitimacy Theory provides the stance for distinguishing description, explanation, and axiology from one another. This distinction is critical in laying bare the value foundations on which decisions are made.

Ferreting out values is frequently a difficult task. However, the EL framework provides the analytic structure to do so. As we proceeded through the book, we identified the descriptive elements and distinguished observables and reportables and looked at the value overlay that creates categories of typicality and atypicality. We also separated description from explanation and provided tools for you to identify and expand explanations. We are left with the values that frame how description and explanation are applied to judgment and response.

There are many methods of value clarification and analysis. We are suggesting, however, that for advancing legitimate communities, methods relying on dialogue and communication among those with disparate views form the foundation for discussions of value. We are not alone in this belief. In an article in the *Chronicle of Higher Education*, Etzioni (2000) identified honest, frank discussion as the primary method to bring groups to mutual understanding and negotiation. Following is a series of questions to guide you in value clarification:

1. What is the scope of your inquiry and of the application of the value set?
2. What is the source of value information (mission statements, legislation, action, individual behavior, rules for group membership, funding and spending patterns)?
3. What is explicitly and/or implicitly desirable? Undesirable? Omitted?
4. What evidence supports the answers to the first three questions?

In our vision of community legitimacy, critical, honest examination of what groups and individuals find desirable and undesirable and the limits of acceptability of human description and explanation would be ongoing.

Consider this example. A federally funded initiative to improve the health and life experience for adolescents with special health care needs, including disabled adolescents, is titled "Healthy and Ready to Work." This title seems to imply value on work and health. Yet in looking at the mandated outcome criteria for this initiative, no direct measures of health are required. Health and medical service use and insurance coverage are central to the evaluation outcome. That is not to say that health is not valued. Yet a careful analysis and discussion identifies the primary value on fiscal support for health services and regular service use as the basis for health.

In the implementation of "Healthy and Ready to Work" projects, the adolescents have identified value on insurance coverage for their health needs, but more important to them was the opportunity for inclusion in their communities along with their nondisabled counterparts. Clearly, two different value sets are operating. In a legitimate community, both groups would communicate, lay out their values, and negotiate how to actualize both value sets and/or compromise.

Self-Determination

We introduced the construct of self-determination earlier in this book. We defined self-determination as the absence of external constraints, the ability and means to direct one's activities, and the power of conscious choice between significant, known alternatives.

In this chapter, we take self-determination further to suggest that it is both an individual and a community right. We assert that respecting the right to self-determination for all individuals in a legitimate community confers not only equal rights but equal responsibilities as well. Moreover, considering community self-determination as a right holds the legitimate community as rightfully entitled to define its boundaries as well as responsible for both those boundaries and those who make up the community.

Let's consider why. If within social and legal boundaries that are respectful of and reflect the diverse human perspectives, knowledge, value, and skill embodied within the community, each individual has the right to choice, it follows that each person then is responsible for those choices. Therefore, we define our vision of community legitimacy as one in which each member, along with the collective, takes responsibility for his or her choices, actions, explanations for those actions, and values regarding explanations.

In such a community, categorical access to resources would not be necessary since, theoretically, all individuals would decide on their contributions with full knowledge of community values. Without the conflict over resources, the importance of who fits within which category would be diminished. It would follow that the control over determining who legitimately does and does not fit (within conceptions of normalcy and worth) would therefore be less important, and multiple perspectives would be acceptable. If categorical access and treatment were decreased and ultimately replaced with notions of difference as respected and expected, then differential response would not occur on the basis of category membership. Moreover, responsibility would be asserted by individual and collective choices and actions. These are the foundations of a community in which categorical worth is replaced by respect for a range of human diversity.

Once again, however, while this vision makes common sense, it is not simple to implement given the differences in humans, human advantage and disadvantage, and so forth. We therefore follow Kelley in his view of social justice informed by past and current failures and future vision. Given the unequal nature of human characteristics, the complimentary capacities of individuals could be planfully integrated to define and achieve community legitimacy.

Let's visit with our four characters in a legitimate community. What do their lives look like?

The way in which Joshua participates in desired work activity is flexible according to how he experiences weakness, vision, and other issues related to the explanations for his atypicality. Rather than asserting that Joshua is sick or too disabled to work, the community has responded with distance technology for telecommuting, flexible hours, and transportation options.

Jennifer balances work, social life, and leisure in a universally accessible community. In older areas of the community in which access is limited, accommodations are readily available. Transportation is universally accessible so that Jennifer, along with all who use it, can transport themselves where and when they want. The obligation for accessible transportation in Jennifer's legitimate community belongs to all, not just to those with atypical mobility.

Marie has just gotten a job as a chef. Her talents as a cook were assessed by the vocational school. She completed her cooking certificate and was then sent to a gourmet school. To address her reading atypicality, she receives support from individuals in her workplace and utilizes accessible cookbooks through technological means.

John has just retired and has been given information about sensory access in his community. This legitimate community is equipped with an FM loop in all public buildings and movie theaters.

SUMMARY

We have suggested specific strategies for change in this chapter. We leave you now with our view of social change as a collaborative effort among individuals who are self-determining and who together hold and share a full complement of skills, knowledge, and values that they bring to advance a progressive community legitimacy agenda.

References

AAMR. (1995–2003). *Definition of mental retardation*. (Updated July 29, 2002). Retrieved January 14, 2003 from *http://www.aamr.org/Policies/faq_mental_retardation.shtml*

ABLEDATA. (n.d.). *Welcome to ABLEDATA, the premier source for information on assistive technology!* Retrieved January 12, 2003 from *http://www.abledata.com/*

Abrams, J. (1998). *Judaism and disability: portrayals in ancient texts from the Tanach through the Bavli*. Washington, D.C.: Gallaudet University Press.

ADAPT. (n.d.). A community-based alternative to nursing homes and institutions for people with disabilities. Retrieved January 12, 2003, from http://www.adapt.org/casaintr.htm

Adorno, T. (1941). *The culture industry: Selected essays on mass culture*. London: Routledge.

Agnes, M. (1999). *Webster's new world college dictionary* (4th ed.). New York, NY: John Wiley and Sons.

Aiello, D. (1986). Issues and concerns confronting disabled assault victims: Strategies for treatment and prevention. *Sexuality and Disability, 7*(3/4), 96–101.

Air Carrier Access Act of 1986 (Public L. No. 99-435, 100 Stat 1080 (1987)).

Architectural Barriers Act, 1968. (42 USC §§ 4151 et seq. § 4151).

Albrecht, G. L., Seelman, K. D., & Bury, M. (Eds.). (2001). *Handbook of disability studies*. Thousand Oaks, CA: Sage.

Allen, B., & Allen, S. (1995). The process of socially constructing mental retardation: Toward value-based interaction. *JASH, 20*, 158–160.

Althusser, L. (1999). *Writings on psychoanalysis (European perspectives: A series in social thought and cultural criticism)*. New York, NY: Columbia University Press.

American Nurses Association. (2002). *About us: ANA's Mission Statement*. Retrieved January 10, 2003 from: *http://nursing world.org/about/mission.htm*.

American Psychiatric Association. (2000). *Diagnostic and statistical manual* (text revision). Washington, D.C.

American Psychiatric Association. (1973). *Diagnostic and statistical manual II* (2nd ed.). Washington, D.C.

American Physical Therapy Association. (2003). *APTA Mission Statement*. Retrieved January 10, 2003 from:*http://www.apta.org/About/aptamissiongoals/aptamissionstatement*

American-Speech-Language-Hearing Association. (1997–2002). Retrieved January 14, 2003 from: *http://www.asha.org/index.cfm*

Americans with Disabilities Act of 1990, PL 101-336, 42 U.S.C. Section 12101 et seq.

Anand, S., & Hanson, K. (1997). Disability adjusted fife years: A critical review. *Journal of Health Economics, 16*, 685–702.

Anspach, R. P. (1979). From stigma to identity politics: Political activism among the physically disabled and former mental patients. *Social Science of Medicine, 13A,* 765–773.

Asch, A. (2001). Disability, bioethics and human rights. In G. L. Albrecht, K. D. Seelman, & M. Bury (Eds.). *Handbook of disability studies* (pp. 397–326). Thousand Oaks, CA: Sage.

Assistive Technology Act of 1998, P. L. 105-394, 29 U.S.C. 3001.

Axinn, J., & Stern, M. (2000). *Social welfare: A history of the American response to need.* Boston, MA: Allyn & Bacon.

Aylward, G. P. (1994). *Practitioner's guide to developing and psychological testing (Critical issues in developmental and behavioral pediatrics).* New York, NY: Plenum.

Barker, C., & Lipson, J. (2002). *You Can't Be Disabled—I Saw You Playing Tennis: Invisibility, Accommodation, and Attitudes about MCS.* Paper presented at Annual Meeting of the Society for Disability Studies. June 7, 2002. Oakland, CA.

Baladerian, N. J. (1991). Sexual abuse of people with developmental disabilities. *Sexuality and Disability, 9,* 323–335.

Barnartt, S., Schriner, K., & Scotch, R. (2001). Advocacy and Political Action. In G. Albrecht, K. D. Seelman, & M. Bury (Eds.), *Handbook of disability studies* (pp. 430–449). Thousand Oaks, CA: Sage.

Barnes, C. (1996). Disability and the Myth of the independent researcher. *Disability & Society, 11,* 107–10.

Barnes, C., & Mercer, G. (1997). *Doing disability research.* Leeds, England: Disability Press.

Barnes, C., Mercer, G., & Shakespeare, T. (1999). *Exploring disability: A sociological introduction.* Cambridge, UK: Polity Press.

Barnett, S., & Scotch, R. (2002). *Disability protests.* Washington, D.C.: Galludet.

Barton, L. (Ed.). (1996). *Disability and society: Emerging issues and insights.* London: Longman.

Bassnett, I. (2001). Health care professionals and their attitudes towards decisions affecting disabled people. In G. Albrecht, K. D. Seelman, & M. Bury (Eds.), Handbook of disability studies (pp. 450–467). Thousand Oaks, CA: Sage.

Bedirhan, T. (Ed.). (2000). *Disability and culture: Universalism and diversity.* Kirkland, WA: Hogrefe & Huber.

Benjamin, W. (1968). *Art in the age of mechanical reproduction. Illuminations.* New York, NY: Harcourt, Brace and World.

Berkowitz, E. D. (1994). A historical preface to the Americans with Disabilities Act. In H. D. Graham (Ed.), *Civil rights in the United States* (pp. 96–119). University Park, PA: The Pennsylvania State University Press.

Bertalanffy, L. V. (1969). *General system theory; foundations, development, applications* (Rev. ed.). New York, NY: G. Braziller.

Biklen, D., 1990, Communication unbound; Autism and praxis. *Harvard Education Review, 60,* 291–314.

Biklen, D., Morton, M., Saha, S., Duncan, J., Hardodottir, M., Karna, E., O'Connor, S., & Rao, S., 1991, I AMN NOT A UTISTIC OH THJE TYP (I am not autistic on the typewriter). *Disability, Handicap & Society, 6,* 161–180.

Braddock, D. (2001, November). *Public financial support for disability programs at the close of the 20th Century* (A working paper). Boulder, CO: Coleman Institute for Cognitive Disabilities, University of Colorado.

Braddock, D. L. & Parish, S. L. (2001). An institutional history of disability. In G. Albrecht, K. D. Seelman, & M. Bury (Eds.), Handbook of disability studies (pp. 11–68). Thousand Oaks, CA: Sage.

Bryce, H. J. (2000). *Financial and strategic management for nonprofit organizations: A comprehensive reference to legal, financial, management, and operations rules and guidelines for nonprofits* (3rd ed.). San Francisco, CA: Jossey-Bass.

Campbell, J. with Moyers, B.D., & Flowers, B.S. (Eds.). (1990). *The power of myth.* New York: NY: Anchor Books.

Carter, B., McGoldrick, M. (Eds.), Ferraro, G. (1989). *The changing family life cycle: A framework for family therapy* (2nd ed.). New York, NY: Prentice Hall.

Charlton, J. I. (1998). *Nothing about us without us: Disability oppression and empowerment.* Berkeley, CA: University of California Press.

Civil Rights Act of 1964, Pub. L. No. 88-352, 78 Stat. 241 (1964).

Coutinho, M. J., & Repp, A. C. (1999). *Inclusion: The integration of students with disabilities.* Belmont, CA: Wadsworth.

Crossley, R. (1992). Getting the words out: Case studies in Facilitated Communication training. *Topics in Language Disorders, 12*(4), 46–59.

Davis, L. J. (2002). *Bending over backwards: Disability, dismodernism, other difficult positions.* New York, NY: New York University Press.

Davis, L. J. (1995). *Enforcing normalcy: Disability, deafness, and the body.* New York, NY: Verso.

Davis, L. J. (2001). Identity politics, disability, and culture. In G. Albrecht, K. D. Seelman, & M. Bury (Eds.), *Handbook of disability studies* (pp. 535–545). Thousand Oaks, CA: Sage.

Delgado, R., & Stefancic, J. (Eds.). (1999). *Critical race theory: The cutting edge.* Philadelphia, PA: Temple University Press.

DePoy, E. (In Press). Reflections on professional practice from a dual stance. *Psychosocial Process, 16*(1).

DePoy, E. (2002, Spring). Will the real definition of disability please stand up. *Psychosocial Process,* 50–54.

DePoy, E., & Gilson, S. F. (2003). *Evaluation practice.* Belmont, CA: Brooks-Cole.

DePoy, E., & Gitlin, L. (1998). *Introduction to research: Understanding and applying multiple strategies* (2nd ed.). St. Louis, MO: Mosby.

DePoy, E., & Werrbach, G. (1996). Successful living placement for adults with disabilities: Considerations for social work practice. *Social Work in Health Care, 23*(4), 21–34.

Derrida, J. (1974). *Of gramatology* (Gayatri Spivack, Trans.). Baltimore, MD: Johns Hopkins University Press.

Doneley, C., & Buckley, S. (1966). *The tyranny of normal: An anthology.* Kent, OH: Kent State Press.

Durant, W. (1991). *Story of philosophy: The lives and opinions of the world's greatest philosophers* (Reissue edition). New York, NY: Pocket Books.

Early, M. B., Neistadt, M. E., & Crepeau, E. B. (Eds.). (1999). *Willard & Spackman's occupational therapy* (9th ed.). Philadelphia, PA: Lippincott-Raven.

Education for All Handicapped Children Act of 1975, PL 94-142, 20 U.S.C. Section 1400 et seq.

Essink, B., & Marie, L. (1999). DALYs in Europe. *Statistical Journal, 16*(1), 19–29.

Etzioni, A. (2000, November 1). Harsh lessons in incivility. *Chronicle of Higher Education,* XLIX (10), (Section 2), B14–B15.

Fair Housing Amendments Act of 1988 (Pub. L. No. 100-430), 102, Stat. 1619.

Fanon, F. (1966). *The wretched of the earth.* New York, NY: Grove Press.

Fawcett, N., & Brantley, M. (2002, June 11). Supreme Court ruling favors worker safety: Case is third this year to limit ADA in the workplace. *iCan News Service.* Retrieved January 12, 2003 from http://www.ican.com/news/fullpage.cfm/articleid/19FAE853-CCF2-4BE4-BB1F199AAD82925E/cx/employment.employment_news/article.cfm

Fine, M., & Asch, A. (1988). Disability beyond stigma: Social interaction, discrimination and activism. *Journal of Social Issues, 44,* 3–21.

Finkelstein, V. (1991). Disability: An administrative challenge? In M. Oliver (Ed.), *Social work, disabled people and disabling environment,* (pp. 19–39).London: Jessica Kingsley.

French, S., & Swain, J. (2001). The relationship between disabled people and health and welfare professionals. In G. Albrecht, K. D. Seelman, & M. Bury (Eds.), *Handbook of disability studies* (pp. 734–753). Thousand Oaks, CA: Sage.

Freud, S. (1978). *Sigmund Freud: His life in pictures and words.* New York, NY: Harcourt Brace Jovanovich.

Friedson, E. (1980). *Doctoring together: A study of professional social control.* Chicago, IL: Chicago University Press.

Fuchs, S. (2001). *Against essentialism: A theory of culture and society.* Cambridge, MA: Harvard University Press.

Fussell, P. (1983). *Class: A painfully accurate guide through the American status system.* New York, NY: Ballantine Books.

Garland-Thomson, R. (Ed.). (1996). *Freakery: Cultural spectacles of the extraordinary body.* New York, NY: New York University Press.

Gill, C. (1997). Four types of integration in disability identity development. *Journal of Vocational Rehabilitation, 9,* 39–46.

Gill, C. (1992, November). Who gets the profits? Workplace oppression devalues the disability experience. *Mainstream, 12,* 14–17.

Gill, C. (1996). Dating and relationship issues. *Sexuality and Disability, 14,* 183–190.

Gilmer, D., DePoy, E., & Meehan, J. (2003). *Perspectives on quality: How long term care users in Maine define quality services: A report of research findings.* Orono, ME: The University of Maine Center for Community Inclusion.

Gilson, S. F. (1998). Case management and supported employment: A good fit. *Journal of Case Management, 7,* 10–17.

Gilson, S. F. (1999). Changing person-environment configurations: Importance of gaining an understanding of the biological system. In E. D. Hutchison (Ed./AU.), *Human Behavior in the Social Environment* (pp. 81–108). Thousand Oaks, CA: Pine Forge.

Gilson, S. F. (1998). Choice and self advocacy: A consumer's perspective. In P. Wehman & J. Kregel (Eds.), *More than a job* (pp. 3–23). Baltimore, MD: Paul H. Brookes.

Gilson, S. F. (2000). Disability and the sick role. In Clifton D. Bryant (Editor-in-Chief). *The Encyclopedia of Criminology and Deviant Behavior.* In C. E. Faupel & P. M. Roman (Eds.), *Volume Four, Self Destructive Behavior and Disvalued Identity* (pp. 184–187). Philadelphia, PA: Taylor & Francis.

Gilson, S. F. (1996). Students with disabilities: An increasing voice and presence on college campuses. *Journal of Vocational Rehabilitation, 6,* 263–272.

Gilson, S. F., Cramer, E. P., & DePoy, E. (2001). (Re)defining abuse among women with disabilities: Enlarging the scope. *AFFILIA, 16,* 220–235.

Gilson & DePoy, E. (In Press). Disability, identity, and cultural diversity. *Disability Studies Quarterly.*

Gilson, S. F., & DePoy, E. (2000). Multiculturalism and disability: A critical perspective. *Disability & Society, 15*(2), 207–218.

Gilson, S. F., & DePoy, E. (2002). Theoretical approaches to disability content in social work education. *Journal of Social Work Education, 37,* 153–165.

Gilson, S. F., Tusler, A., & Gill, C. J. (1997). Ethnographic research in disability identity: Self-determination and community. *Journal of Vocational Rehabilitation, 9,* 7–17.

Gitlow, L. (2001). Occupational therapy attitudes toward the inclusion of students with disabilities in their educational programs. *Occupational Therapy Journal of Research, 21,* 115–131.

Gleeson, B. J. (1997). Disability studies: A historical materialist view. *Disability and Society, 12,* 179–202.

Goldberg, D. T. (1994). *Multiculturalism: A critical reader.* Oxford, England: Blackwell.

Gould, S. J. (1996). *The mismeasure of man.* New York, NY: W. W. Norton.

Gutmann, A., & Appiah, K. A. (1998). *Color conscious.* Princeton, NJ: Princeton University Press.

Hahn, H. (1991). Alternative views of empowerment: Social services and civil rights. *Journal of Rehabilitation, 57,* 17–19.

Hahn, H. (1993). The politics of physical differences: Disability and discrimination, In M. Nagler (Ed.), *Perspectives on disability* (2nd ed., pp. 37–42). Palo Alto, CA: Health Markets Research.

Hanson, B. (2002). Inequalities created in bio-medicine as the body business. In J. J. Kronenfeld (Ed.), *Social inequities, health and health care delivery.* Oxford, UK: Elsevier Press.

Harkin, T. (1990, July 26). News Release: Overview of the Americans with Disabilities Act of 1990.

Harrison. L. E., & Huntington, S. P. (Eds.). (2000). *Culture matters: How values shape human progress.* New York, NY: Basic Books.

Harris, L., & Associates. (1998). *1998 N.O.D./Harris survey of Americans with disabilities.* Washington, D.C.: National Organization on Disability.

Harris, L. & Associates. (1986). *The ICD survey of disabled Americans: Bringing disabled Americans into the mainstream.* New York, NY: ICD—International Center for the Disabled.

Hartman, A., DePoy, E., Francis, C., & Gilmer, D. (2000). Adolescents with special health care needs in transition: Three life histories. (2002). *Social Work & Health Care, 31*(4), 3–58.

Heumann, J. E. (1993). Building our own boats: A personal perspective on disability policy. In L. O. Gostin & H. A. Beyer (Eds.), *Implementing the Americans with Disabilities Act: Rights and responsibilities of all Americans* (pp. 251–262). Baltimore, MD: Paul H. Brookes.

Higgins, P. C. (1992). *Making disability: Exploring the social transformation of human variation.* Springfield, IL: Charles C. Thomas.

Higgins, R. C. (2000). *Analysis for financial management.* New York, NY: McGraw-Hill.

Holstein, M., & Cole, T. R. (1996). The evolution of long-term care in America. In R. H. Binstock, L. E. Cluff, & O. Von Mering (Eds.), *The future of long-term care: Social and policy issues* (pp. 19–47). Baltimore, MD: Johns Hopkins University Press.

Hutchison, E. D. (1993). Mandatory reporting laws: child protective case finding gone awry? *Social-Work, 38*(1), 56–63.

Hutchison, E. D. (1999). *Dimensions of human behavior.* Thousand Oaks, CA: Pine Forge Press.

iCan! (1999–2002). *Disability resource links.* Retrieved January 12, 2003, from *http://www.ican.com/channels/resources.cfm*

Ingstad, B., & Whyte, S. R. (1995). *Disability and culture.* Berkley, CA: University of California Press.

Jameson, F., & Miyoshi, M. (2001). *The cultures of globalization.* Durham, NC: Duke University Press.

Jost, J. T., Major, B. (2002). *The psychology of legitimacy: emerging perspectives on ideology, justice, and intergroup relations.* Cambridge, U.K.: Cambridge University Press.

Kane, R. A., Kane, R. L. & Ladd, R. C. (1998). *The heart of long-term care.* New York, NY: Oxford University Press.

Kanigel, R. (1999). *The one best way: Frederick Winslow Taylor and the enigma of efficiency* (Sloan Technology Series). New York, NY: Viking Press.

Katz, M. B. (1996). In The Shadow of the Poorhouse: A Social History of Welfare in America. New York, NY: BasicBooks.

Kaufman, A. S. (1994). *Intelligence testing with the Wisc-III* (Wiley Series on Personality Processes). New York, NY: Wiley.

Kelley, R. D. G. (2002, June 7). Finding the strength to love and dream. *Chronicle of Higher Education, LVIII* (39) (Section 2), B7–B9.

Kielhofner, G. (Ed.). (2002). *A model of human occupation: Theory and application* (3rd ed.). Baltimore, MD: Lippincott Williams & Wilkins Publishers.

Kirst-Ashman, K. K., & Hull, G. H. (2001). *Understanding generalist practice/with Infotrak.* Pacific Grove, CA: Wadsworth.

Kohlberg, L. (1984). *The psychology of moral development.* New York, NY: Harper and Row.

Kothari, V. N., & Gulati, I. S. (1997). Disability-adjusted life year as a guide for health-policy. *Economic and Political Weekly, 32*(41), 2612–2617.

Kymlicka, W. (1995). *Multicultural citizenship.* New York, NY: Oxford University Press.

Lacey, M. (2002, June 15). Fighting 'Light Skin' as a standard of beauty. New York Times.

Langer, W. L., Geanakaplos, D. J., Hexter, J. H., & Pipes, R. (Eds.). (1975). *Western civilization, V1&2.* (2nd ed.). New York, NY: Harper & Row.

Law, M. C., Baum, C., & Dunn, W. (2000). *Measuring occupational performance: Supporting best practice in occupational therapy.* Thorofare, NJ: Slack.

Levine, L. W. (1990). *Highbrow/lowbrow: The emergence of cultural hierarchy in America* (Reprint ed.). Cambridge, MA: Harvard University Press.

Levi-Strauss, C. (2000). *Structural anthropology.* New York, NY: Basic Books.

Levitas, A. S., & Reid, C. S. (2003). An angel with Down syndrome in a sixteenth century Flemish Nativity painting. *American Journal of Medical Genetics* Published Online: 11 Dec 2002.

Liebow, E. (1967). *Tally's corner.* Boston, MA: Little Brown.

Linton, S. (1998). *Claiming disability: Knowledge and identity.* New York, NY: New York University Press.

Longmore, P. K. (1995). The second phase: From disability rights to disability culture. *Disability Rag ReSource,* September/October, 4–11.

Longmore, P. K., & Umansky, L. (Eds.). (2001). *The new disability history: American perspectives (History of disability).* New York, NY: New York University Press.

Mackelprang, R. W., & Salsgiver, R. O. (1999). *Disability: A diversity model approach in human service practice.* Pacific Grove, CA: Brooks Cole.

Majid, A. (2002, November 1) The failure of post-colonial theory after 9/11. *Chronicle of Higher Education, XLIX* (10), (Section 2), B11–12.

McLaughlin, M. J., Schofield, P. E., & Warren, S. H. (1999). Educational reform: Issues for the inclusion of students with disabilities. In M. J. Coutino & A. C. Repp (Eds.), *Inclusion: The integration of students with disabilities* (pp. 37–58). Belmont, CA: Wadsworth.

Minkel, J. R. (2002). A way with words. *Scientific American, 25*(March). Retrieved June 25, 2002, from: *www.scientificamerican.com/explorations/2002*

Mitchell, D. T., & Snyder, S. L. (2001). Representation and its discontents: The uneasy home of disability in literature and film. In G. Albrecht, K. D. Seelman, & M. Bury (Eds.), *Handbook of disability studies* (pp. 194–218). Thousand Oaks, CA: Sage.

Moller-Okin, S. (with respondents). (1999). *Is multiculturalism bad for women? Princeton, NJ: Princeton University Press.*

Moller-Okin, S. (1999). *Is multiculturalism bad for women?* Princeton, NJ: Princeton University Press.

Morse, J. M., & Fields, P. A. (1995). *Qualitative Research Methods for Health Professionals* (2nd ed.). Thousand Oaks, CA: Sage.

Murray, C. J. L., & Acharya, A. K. (1997). Understanding DALYs. *Journal of Health Economics, 16,* 703–30.

Mussen, P. (1983). *Handbook of child psychology.* New York, NY: Wiley.

National Coalition Against Domestic Violence. (1996). *Open minds, open doors.* Denver, CO: Author.

National Organization on Disability. (2000). *Key findings: 2000 N.O.D./Harris Survey of Americans with Disabilities.* Retrieved on February 20, 2003 from www.nod.org/

Netting, E. Kettner, P. M., & McMurty, S. E. (1998). *Social work macro practice.* New York, NY: Longman.

Nosek, M. A., Howland, C. A., & Young, M. E. (1997). Abuse of women with disabilities: Policy implications. *Journal of Disability Policy Studies, 8,* 157–175.

O'Brien, J., &. O'Brien, C. L. (Eds.), (1997). *A little book about person-centered planning: Ways to think about person-centered planning, its limitations, the conditions for its success and its contributions to organizational renewal.* Toronto, Ontario, Canada: Inclusion Press.

Oliver, M. (1992). Changing the social relations of research production? *Disability, Handicap, & Society, 7*(2), 101–14.

Oliver, M. (1996a). Defining impairment and disability: Issues at stake. In G. Barnes & G. Mercer (Eds.), *Exploring the divide: Illness and disability* (pp. 39–54). Leeds, United Kingdom: The Disability Press.

Oliver, M. (1996b). *Understanding disability: From theory to practice.* New York, NY: St. Martin's Press.

Parsons, T. (1956). *Economy and society: A study in the integration of economic and social theory.* Glencoe, IL: Free Press.

Percy, S. (1989). *Disability, civil rights, and public policy: The politics of implementation.* Tuscaloosa, AL: University of Alabama Press.

Pfeiffer, D. (1998). ICHD: And the need for its revision. *Disability and Society, 13,* 503–523.

Pfeiffer, D. (2002). Philosophical foundations of disability. *Disability Studies Quarterly, 22*(2), 3–22.

Quinn, P. (1998). *Understanding disability: A lifespan approach.* Thousand Oaks, CA: Sage.

Ravaud, J., & Stiker, H. (2001). Inclusion/exclusion: An analysis of historical and cultural meanings. In G. L. Albrecht, K. D. Seelman, & M. Bury (Eds.), *Handbook of disability studies* (pp. 490–512). Thousand Oaks, CA: Sage.

Rehabilitation Act of 1973, PL 93-112, 29 U.S.C. Section 701 et seq.

Rioux, M. H. (1994). New research directions and paradigms: Disability is not measles. In M. H. Rioux & M. Bach (Eds.), *Disability is not measles: New research paradigms in disability* (pp. 1–7). North York, Ontario: Roeher Institute.

Rogers, M. F. & Ritzer, G. (Eds.). (1996). *Multicultural experiences, multicultural theories.* New York, NY: McGraw-Hill.

Russell, M. (1998). *Beyond ramps*. Monroe, ME: Common Courage Press.

Sands, D. J., & Wehmeyer, M. L. (1996). *Self Determination across the lifespan*. Baltimore, MD: Paul Brookes.

Schriner, K. F., & Scotch, R. K. (1998). Beyond the minority group model: Am emerging paradigm for the next generation of disability policy. In E. Makas, B. Haller, & T. Doe (Eds.), *Accessing the issues: Current research in disability studies* (pp. 213–216). Dallas, TX: The Society for Disability Studies and The Edmund S. Muskie Institute of Public Affairs.

Scotch, R. K. (2001). *From goodwill to civil rights: Transforming federal disability policy* (2nd ed.). Philadelphia, PA: Temple University Press.

Scotch, R. K. (1989). Politics and policy in the history of the disability rights movement. *Milbank Quarterly, 67*(2) (Suppl. 2), 380–400.

Scotch, R., & Schriner, K. (1997). Disability as human variation: Implications for policy. *The Annals of the American Academy of Political and Social Science, 549,* 148–160.

Shakespeare, T. (1996). Disability, identity and difference. In G. Barnes & G. Mercer (Eds.), *Exploring the divide: Illness and disability* (pp. 94–113). Leeds, United Kingdom: The Disability Press.

Shakespeare, T., & Watson, N. (1997). Defending the social model. *Disability and Society, 12,* 293–300.

Shapiro, J. P. (1990). *No pity: People with disabilities forging a new civil rights movement*. New York, NY: Times Books.

Silvers, A., Wasserman, D., & Mahowald, M. B. (1998). *Disability, difference, discrimination: Perspectives on justice in bioethics and public policy*. Lanham, MD: Rowman & Littlefield.

Sobsey, D., & Doe, T. (1991). Patterns of sexual abuse and assault. *Sexuality and Disability, 9,* 243–259.

Starr, P. (1984). *Social transformation of American medicine* (Reprint ed.). New York: Basic Books.

Starr, P. (1982). *Transformation of American medicine*. New York, NY: Basic Books.

Stiker, H. J. (2000). *A history of disability (Corporealities)*. Ann Arbor, MI: University of Michigan Press.

Stone, D. A. (1986). *The disabled state*. Philadelphia, PA: Temple University Press.

Stone, D. A. (2002). *Policy paradox: The art of political decision making* (Revised ed.). New York, NY: W. W. Norton.

Storey, J. (Ed.). (1998). *Cultural theory and popular culture: A reader* (2nd ed.). Athens, GA: University of Georgia Press.

Swain, J., Finkelstein, V., French, S., & Oliver, M. (Eds.). (1993). *Disabling barriers— Enabling environments*. London, UK: Sage.

Technology-Related Assistance for Individuals with Disabilities Act of 1988 (Tech Act).

Thyer, B. (2001). *The handbook of social work research methods*. Thousand Oaks, CA: Sage.

Treanor, R. B. (1993). *We overcame: The story of civil rights for disabled people*. Falls Church, VA: Regal Direct.

United States Census Bureau. (2002). *Americans with disabilities, 1997*. Report issued by United States Census Bureau. Retrieved December 20, 2002, from http://landview.census.gov/hhes/www/disable/sipp/disable97.html

Ustun, T. B., Catterji, S., Rehm, J., Shekhar, S., Bickenbach, J. E., Trotter, R. T., & Room, R. (2002). *Disability and culture: Universalism and diversity*. Seattle, WA: Hogrefe & Huber.

Violence Against Women Act of 2000 (P.L. 106-386), enacted on October 28, 2000.

VISA. (1996–2001). About VISA: Sponsorships. Visa Sponsors the ATHENS 2004 Paralympic Games. Retrieved January 12, 2003 from http: *http://international. visa.com/av/sponsorhips/paralympics/main.jsp*

Vocational Education Act of 1917 (Public L. 63-347, 39 Stat. 929)

Walter, L. J. (1988). *Abused women with disabilities: Prevalence and profiles.* Paper presentation at 8th National Conference and 20 Year Anniversary of the National Coalition Against Domestic Violence. Denver, CO.

Walzer, M. (1994, Spring). Multiculturalism & individualism. *Dissent, 41*(2), 185–191.

Wehman, P. (Ed.) (2001). Supported employment in business: Expanding the capacity of workers with disabilities. St. Augustine, FL: Training Resource Network.

Weitz, R. (2001). *The sociology of health, illness, and health care: A critical approach* (2nd ed.). Belmont, CA: Wadsworth.

WE Magazine. (2002). Retrieved January 12, 2003 from *http://www.wemagazine.com/*

Winzer, M. A. (1997). Disability and society: Before the 18th Century: Dread and dispare. In L. J. Davis (Ed.), *Disability studies reader* (pp. 75–109). New York, NY: Routledge.

Wright, B. A. (1988). Attitudes and the fundamental negative bias: Conditions and corrections. In H. E. Yuker (Ed.), *Attitudes toward persons with disabilities* (pp. 3–21). New York, NY: Springer.

Young, M. E., Nosek, M. A., Howland, C., Chanpong, G., & Rintala, D. H. (1997). Prevalence of abuse of women with physical disabilities. *Archives of Physical Medicine and Rehabilitation, 78,* Suppl 5, S34–S38.

Yzerbyt, V., & Rogier, A. (2001). Blame it on the group: Entitativity, subjective essentialism, and social attribution. In J. T. Jost & B. Major (Eds.), *The psychology of legitimacy: Emerging perspectives on ideology, justice, and intergroup relations* (pp. 103–134). Cambridge, UK: Cambridge University Press.

Zola, I. K. (1993). Self, identity and the naming question: Reflections on the language of disability. In M. Nagler (Ed.), *Perspectives on disability* (2nd ed., pp. 15–23). Palo Alto, CA: Health Markets Research.

Glossary

Appearance   How people look to others.

Activity   What people do, how they do it, and what they do not do throughout their lives.

Atypicality   That which is odd, different, or infrequent.

Description   The full range of human activity, appearance and experience.

Dissent anxiety   A resistive and alienating response that proponents of civil rights movements express when the notion of group or cultural identity is questioned or challenged.

Diversity depth   Reportables of difference.

Diversity patina   Observables of difference.

Experience   The reportable element of description; one's personal and unique ways of being, articulating, and sensing.

Observables   Activities and appearances; claims that can be verified with directly experienced information.

Personal stance   The unique vantage point from which one observes and interprets; includes one's experience, knowledge, theoretical lens, beliefs, values, and purposes.

Reportables   Inferred claims.

Typicality   That which is usual and frequent.

Undisabling   The removal of a disabling factor or set of factors.

Index